A Practical Course in Horology

A PRACTICAL COURSE IN HOROLOGY

A
PRACTICAL COURSE
IN
HOROLOGY

By HAROLD C. KELLY

Head, Department of Horology
Southwestern Institute of Technology
Weatherford, Oklahoma

THE MANUAL ARTS PRESS
PEORIA, ILLINOIS

CONTENTS

PART III: ADJUSTING

TIME

BY *Laurens L. Simpson*

(WRITTEN TO ACCOMPANY THE GIFT OF A WATCH)

•

I am time.
I come to give thee life
Twenty-four hours of every day,
All this to every man.

I tick tick.
I sound in peace, and strife,
In sleep, in work and play,
Forever, on and on.

I never change
To good and bad alike.
The rich, the brave, the free
All use me as they may.

I am gold
To those who will; to others
Lead, who do not see
The benefit of industry.

I am power.
Weak to strong, coward to brave,
Man grows as I move on,
Or not, as will he may.

(CONTINUED NEXT PAGE)

7

I am fame
To those whose light is bright,
Who shine with all their might,
Pure, through day and night.

I am happiness
To those who serve and give,
Who help the weak, make known
The unknown, and live.

Now or never
Equal chance I give to all,
My days to use or lose,
Here once then gone forever.

PREFACE

THE ART of horology unquestionably ranks among the most wonderful of the mechanical arts. One can only marvel at the diminutive size of the modern wrist watch and the accuracy of the machines by which the duplicate parts are made.

Production and improved manufacturing methods have also changed the repairman's approach to horology. Duplicate parts are available, so the horologist is seldom called upon to make a part. However, since the sizes of watches have been reduced, new tools and improved methods are essential to good workmanship. One must develop a greater skill in fitting staffs to small, uncut balance wheels, in adjusting small escapements, and in handling the new, alloyed balance springs.

The purpose of this book is to present the fundamentals of horology, both in theory and practice. *Part 1* deals with wheel work and gearing, which involve the work of calculating the number of teeth of missing wheels and pinions and in determining their proper diameters. Principles of escapement design and an analysis of the balance and spring are given considerable space. *Part 2* treats repair methods, in which the making of a balance staff and the adjustment of the escapement are given more than the usual space allotted to these subjects. *Part 3* is concerned with the adjustments to position, isochronism, and temperature, factors that

9

may be called the finishing touches of the horological profession.

The author is indebted to T. J. Wilkinson and C. E. DeLong for the reading of parts of the manuscript and for helpful suggestions. The chapter on wheel work is based on a system by Jules Grossman, late director of the horological school of Locle.

It is hoped that this work will contribute some small part toward the development of a generation of capable and well equipped horologists.

HAROLD C. KELLY

PART 1

GENERAL PRINCIPLES

CHAPTER ONE

Wheel Work

Terminology

WHEEL WORK is the basis for the construction of all instruments for the registering of time. Even the clepsydra, one of the earliest forms of a clock, which operated by the dripping of water, involved the use of wheels. The wheels of these early clocks as well as those of the first pendulum clocks were filed out by hand and although the workmanship on some of the later creations was quite skillfully executed, they were, of course, very crude as compared with the machine-made wheels of modern clocks and watches. Since wheels are fundamental to the construction of watches, we have decided that this opening chapter shall be given over to the consideration of wheels as they apply to the science of horology. Below are listed several definitions relative to the subject:

Wheel: any circular piece of metal on the periphery of which teeth may be cut of various forms and numbers.

Pinion: the smaller wheel with teeth called *leaves*, working in connection with a larger wheel.

Train: a combination of two or more wheels and pinions, geared together and transmitting power from one part of a mechanism to another.

Barrel: a circular box of metal for the reception of the main spring.

Balance: the vibratory wheel, which, in connection with the balance spring, controls the movement of the hands.

Balance spring: a fine, coiled wire, one end of which is attached by a *collet* to the *balance staff* and the other end to some stationary part of the watch through the medium of a piece called a *stud*.

Beat: one vibration of the balance and balance spring resulting from an impulse received by means of an escapement.

Escapement: includes those parts of a watch which change the circular force of the escape wheel into the vibratory motion of the balance

Pallets: that part of an escapement which receives impulse from the escape wheel and by means of a lever delivers impulse to the balance. This term includes the pallet arms and jewels.

Receiving pallet: that pallet stone over which a tooth of the escape wheel slides in order to enter between the pallet stones.

Discharging pallet: that pallet stone over which a tooth of the escape wheel slides in order to leave from between the pallets.

Lock: the overlapping contact of an escape wheel tooth on a pallet stone's locking face

Watch Trains

Since the motive force stored in the main spring of a watch does not act directly on the balance, it is by necessity transmitted by a system of toothed wheels and pinions. This system of wheels and pinions, commonly called a train, is a scientific, mathematical assemblage of mobiles, and anyone who becomes familiar with the principles involved derives much satisfaction from such knowledge.

In watches we have two trains, the main train and the dial train. The *main train* changes a slow motion into a fast one with the particular purpose of causing the wheel that carries the minute hand to make one turn in the same time that the escapement makes a required number of beats.

The *dial train,* on the other hand, changes a fast motion into a slow one for the purpose of governing the distance the hour hand travels to one turn of the minute hand.

The Main Train

Calculating the number of turns of a pinion. In order to obtain the number of turns of a pinion into which a wheel is geared, we divide the number of teeth in the wheel by the number of leaves in the pinion. Suppose, for example, a wheel of 72 teeth gears into a pinion of 12 leaves. Designating the wheel as *B* and the pinion into which the wheel gears as *c,* Figure 1, the formula for the problem reads as follows:

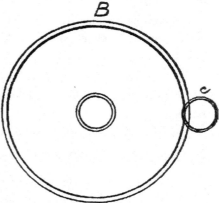

Figure 1.

$$\frac{B}{c} = \text{number of turns of the pinion.}$$

Substituting $\dfrac{B}{c}$ by their numerical values we have:

$$\frac{72}{12} = 6 \text{ turns of the pinion to one of the wheel.}$$

Calculating the number of turns of a complete train.
Most watch trains contain five wheels, as shown in Figure 2.
These include the main-spring barrel and the escape wheel,
and all five mobiles are usually named as follows:

B = barrel or first wheel
C = center or second wheel
T = third wheel
F = fourth wheel
E = escape wheel

The pinions are as follows:

c = center or second pinion
t = third pinion
f = fourth pinion
e = escape pinion

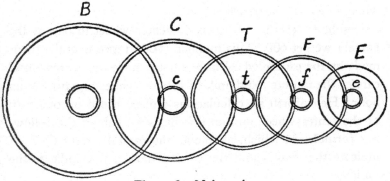

Figure 2. Main train.

It will be noted that the second pinion is in reality the first pinion, but for convenience it is given the same name as the wheel of which it is a part and referred to as the center or second pinion.

As an example of a modern train we shall select the number of teeth of wheels and leaves of pinions as shown below. (Remember, the barrel, center, third, fourth and escape wheels are indicated by the capital letters B, C, T, F and E, and the center, third, fourth and escape pinions by the small letters c, t, f and e.)

$$\frac{B}{c} = \frac{72}{12} = 6$$

$$\frac{C}{t} = \frac{80}{10} = 8$$

$$\frac{T}{f} = \frac{75}{10} = 7\frac{1}{2}$$

$$\frac{F}{e} = \frac{80}{8} = 10$$

Multiplying the numbers 6, 8, 7½, and 10 together we get 3,600, which represents the number of turns of the escape wheel to one of the barrel.

Dividing 3,600 by 6 (turns of center wheel to one of the barrel) we get 600. This number (600) represents the turns made by the escape wheel in one hour, since the center wheel carries the minute hand and, of course, makes one turn in an hour. Henceforth all calculations will be based on one turn of the center wheel, and on this basis we submit the following formula, in which, as above, the capital letters C, T, F indicate the wheels and the small letters t, f, e indicate the pinions.

$$\frac{CTF}{tfe} = \frac{80 \times 75 \times 80}{10 \times 10 \times 8} = 600 \text{ turns of the escape wheel.}$$

The fourth wheel in all watches designed to register seconds is so constructed that a second hand is fitted to the extremity of a long pivot extending through a hole in the dial. It follows, therefore, that according to the accepted plan for the division of time, the fourth wheel must make 60 turns to one of the center wheel. Therefore:

$$\frac{CT}{tf} = \frac{80 \times 75}{10 \times 10} = 60 \text{ turns of the fourth wheel.}$$

However, this is not necessary in watches where there is no second hand, and in many wrist watches the fourth wheel makes more than 60 turns to one of the center wheel, as we shall soon see.

Calculating the number of beats. The escape wheel in most watches contains 15 teeth and delivers twice as many impulses to the balance, since each tooth delivers two impulses, first to the receiving pallet and later to the discharging pallet. Letting E indicate the escape wheel and e the escape pinion, the formula reads:

$$\frac{CTF2E}{tfe} = \text{number of beats per hour.}$$

Substituting the numerical values we have:

$$\frac{80 \times 75 \times 80 \times 2 \times 15}{10 \times 10 \times 8} = 18{,}000 \text{ beats per hour.}$$

Fast and slow trains. Not all watches make 18,000 beats per hour. Some of the older watches make 16,200 and 14,400 beats per hour, whereas some newer American wrist watches make 19,800 and 21,600 beats per hour. There are other trains of varying beats per hour, particularly among those of Swiss manufacture. Below are shown two examples of slow trains:

$$\frac{80 \times 75 \times 72 \times 2 \times 15}{10 \times 10 \times 8} = 16{,}200 \text{ beats per hour.}$$

$$\frac{80 \times 75 \times 80 \times 2 \times 15}{10 \times 10 \times 10} = 14{,}400 \text{ beats per hour.}$$

As already stated, watches without second hands may have any system of mobiles wherein the fourth wheel will not register seconds. Below are listed three trains of this type, all of which are fast trains used in small wrist watches.

$$\frac{54 \times 50 \times 48 \times 2 \times 15}{6 \times 6 \times 6} = 18{,}000 \text{ beats per hour.}$$

$$\frac{64 \times 66 \times 60 \times 2 \times 15}{8 \times 8 \times 6} = 19{,}800 \text{ beats per hour.}$$

$$\frac{42 \times 42 \times 35 \times 35 \times 2 \times 12}{7 \times 7 \times 7 \times 7} = 21{,}600 \text{ beats per hour.}$$

The last train listed is unique in that the train has 6 wheels with an escape wheel containing 12 teeth.

Comments on the fast trains. In the preceding paragraphs we discussed the slow and fast trains that have been in general use at various periods. We shall now consider further the modern fast trains used to some extent in very small wrist watches.

The watch train making 18,000 beats per hour has been accepted as a sort of standard for many years. However, very small wrist watches making beats of various numbers per hour in excess of this figure are becoming more in evidence and the increased use of such trains would lead one to inquire into the reason for their popularity

The reason lies in the fact that 18,000-beat trains, when applied to very small wrist watches, have a tendency to set on the locking. This is due to the fact that a light balance and a weak balance spring have not the necessary force to effect a satisfactory unlocking of the escapement. To overcome this fault of setting on the locking, it is necessary to reduce the drop lock to the very minimum. However, since it is difficult to expect the same precision of adjustment in small watches as is possible in larger watches, the fast trains offer a solution. The fast trains make the unlocking easier due to two factors: (1) the more rapid motion of the balance and (2) the increased strength of the balance spring. In this way the new fast trains permit a greater tolerance with regard to the extent of the lock, resulting in a reduced tendency to set on the locking. Better timekeeping results.

There is another point in favor of the new fast trains. Every horologist has observed how often the coils of the balance spring get caught in the regulator pins or get badly tangled due to a severe jolt. The stronger springs fitted to fast train watches do much to eliminate the difficulty or, at least, to lessen its frequent occurrence.

Calculating the number of teeth and leaves of missing mobiles. We now wish to determine the number of teeth of wheels and leaves of pinions that are missing. Let F indicate the missing fourth wheel of the following train:

$$\frac{80 \times 75 \times F \times 2 \times 15}{10 \times 10 \times 8} = 18,000$$

$$225F = 18,000$$

$$F = 80$$

According to the above solution the fourth wheel contains 80 teeth.

In the next problem, the third pinion is mission. Letting t indicate the mission pinion, the equation reads as follows:

$$\frac{80 \times 75 \times 80 \times 2 \times 15}{t \times 10 \times 8} = 18,000$$

$$\frac{180,000}{t} = 18,000$$

$$180,000 = 18,000\,t$$

$$18,000\,t = 180,000$$

$$t = 10 \text{ leaves of the third pinion}$$

Let us suppose that the complete fourth wheel and pinion of a wrist watch are missing in which F is the wheel and f is the pinion. The equation reads:

$$\frac{54 \times 50 \times F \times 2 \times 15}{6 \times f \times 6} = 18,000$$

$$\frac{2,250\,F}{f} = 18,000$$

$$\frac{F}{f} = \frac{18,000}{2,250} = \frac{8}{1}$$

The result shows that the fourth wheel should have 8 times as many teeth as the fourth pinion has leaves. Designating f by 6, 7, 8, or 10 leaves, we may obtain any of the following solutions.

$$\frac{48}{6}; \frac{56}{7}; \frac{64}{8}; \frac{80}{10}$$

Any of the solutions given above may be used; however, judging from the numbers of teeth and leaves of the train as a whole, the most suitable numbers would be:

$$\frac{F}{f} = \frac{48}{6}$$

There are times when the ratios come out with a fractional numerator. For example we wish to determine the number of teeth and leaves of a missing third wheel and pinion in which T is the wheel and t is the pinion.

$$\frac{54 \times T \times 48 \times 2 \times 15}{t \times 6 \times 6} = 18,000$$

$$\frac{2,160T}{t} = 18,000$$

$$\frac{T}{t} = \frac{18,000}{2,160} = \frac{8\frac{1}{3}}{1}$$

The only numbers that may be tried without producing a fractional number of teeth are

$$\frac{75}{9} \text{ and } \frac{50}{6}$$

In this example the most suitable numbers would be:

$$\frac{T}{t} = \frac{50}{6}$$

There are other times when we arrive at the answer immediately, as in the case of determining the number of the teeth of the escape wheel, E, and the leaves of the escape pinion, e.

$$\frac{90 \times 80 \times 80 \times 2E}{12 \times 10 \times e} = 18,000$$

$$\frac{9,600E}{e} = 18,000$$

$$\frac{E}{e} = \frac{18,000}{9,600} = \frac{15}{8}$$

The answer shows that the escape wheel contains 15 teeth and the escape pinion 8 leaves.

Calculating a new train. We now wish to determine the number of teeth for the wheels and number of leaves for the pinions of a new train. Let us suppose the watch is to be a small baguette making 21,600 beats per hour. Using the same letters as before to indicate the wheels and pinions the formula reads as follows:

$$\frac{CTF2E}{tfe} = 21{,}600$$

We may decide in advance the number of leaves for the pinions and the number of teeth for the escape wheel. For the pinions t, f, and e we shall use 6 leaves each. The escape wheel will have 15 teeth. The equation now reads:

$$\frac{CTF\,2 \times 15}{6 \times 6 \times 6} = 21{,}600$$

$$CTF = \frac{21{,}000 \times 6 \times 6 \times 6}{2 \times 15}$$

$$CTF = 155{,}520$$

The combined product of *CTF* is 155,520. In order to obtain the quantities desired, it is necessary to resolve this number into its prime factors and to form these factors into three groups which will represent the numbers for the teeth of the wheels *C, T,* and *F.*

2)155520	2) 9720	3) 405
2) 77760	2) 4860	3) 135
2) 38880	2) 2430	3) 45
2) 19440	3) 1215	3) 15
		5

Factoring, we find that CTF $= 155{,}520 = 2^7 \times 3^5 \times 5$.

These factors may be formed into groups of various combinations, but the most suitable arrangement for a watch train would be as follows:

$$C = 5 \times 3 \times 2^2 = 60$$
$$T = 3^3 \times 2 = 54$$
$$F = 3 \times 2^4 = 48$$

Thus we show the complete train.

$$\frac{60 \times 54 \times 48 \times 2 \times 15}{6 \times 6 \times 6} = 21{,}600 \text{ beats per hour.}$$

The Barrel and Its Mainspring

The barrel and its mainspring are important factors in the design of a watch. The ratio between the barrel and center pinion must show a definite relationship to the length and strength of the mainspring and must be determined with mathematical exactness if the watch is to perform satisfactorily and run a required number of hours.

Calculating the number of hours a given watch will run. In order to determine the number of hours a watch will run we must first find the number of turns of the center wheel to one of the barrel. Letting B indicate the barrel and c the center pinion, the formula reads

$$\frac{B}{c} = \text{number of turns of center wheel to one of the barrel.}$$

Using a numerical example, we have:

$$\frac{84}{12} = 7 \text{ turns of center wheel.}$$

Knowing that the center wheel makes one turn in an hour, it follows that the barrel makes one turn in 7 hours Next we must determine the number of turns necessary to completely wind the spring. A trial has shown that it takes 5½ turns to wind the spring. The number of hours the watch will run is found by multiplying 7 by 5½, thus:

$7 \times 5\frac{1}{2} = 38\frac{1}{2}$ hours the watch will run.

The mainspring should run the watch not less than 32 hours; 36 to 40 hours is better; in fact, some of the finest watches will run 45 hours and more.

Calculating the correct thickness of the mainspring. We experience no difficulty in fitting mainsprings to standard makes of watches, for all we have to do is to select the spring as catalogued and graded by the particular manufacturer. There are times, however, when an old watch or one of unfamiliar make needs a new spring and, if we suspect that the old spring is not the correct one, we need to apply a bit of mathematical calculation to determine the correct thickness of the spring. In such cases the following method is suggested:

1. Divide the teeth of the barrel by the leaves of the center pinion in order to determine the number of hours taken for one turn of the barrel.

2. Determine the number of turns necessary to wind the spring by dividing 36 (hours of running) by the number of hours consumed in one turn of the barrel

3. Measure the inside diameter of the barrel and divide by 12.5.

4 Divide the above quotient by the number of turns necessary to wind the spring. The result is the thickness of the spring.

Suppose for example that the barrel, *B*, has 78 teeth and

the center pinion, *c,* has 12 leaves. The inside diameter of the barrel is 12 millimeters.

1. $\dfrac{B}{c} = \dfrac{78}{12} = 6.5 \times 1 = 6.5$ hours.

2. $\dfrac{36}{6.5} = 5.5$ turns to wind spring.

3. $\dfrac{12}{12.5} = .96$

4. $\dfrac{.96}{5.5} = .17$ mm., thickness of the spring.

It should be understood that the answers are only approximate. In some cases, as in a fine, 21- or 23-jewel watch, a weaker spring may be needed, whereas a 7-jewel watch may require a stronger spring

Calculating the correct length of the mainspring. The proper length of the spring need not be calculated in so many inches. Instead, we may state that the spring should occupy one half of the *area* between the inside wall of the barrel and the periphery of the arbor. If the spring does this, the length is correct.

Observe that we say area and not space. The term space would lead one to infer that radial measurements are intended, which would be incorrect, inasmuch as a spring wound up would occupy more radial space than that of a spring run down. Thus, the statement often found in older books on horology to the effect that we allow one third of the space for the arbor, one third for the space, and one third for the spring is slightly in error and indicative of a spring a few coils too long.

The correct rule should read·

One third of the space is occupied by the barrel arbor and one half of the remaining area is covered by the spring.

This is clearly shown in Figure 3. It will be observed that the radial distance occupied by the spring is less than

Figure 3.   Barrel showing correct space for mainspring.

that given to space. However the area of both spring and space are equal and it remains the same under all conditions, whether the spring is wound completely, partially let down, or completely let down.

Now wind the spring in the barrel and if the spring occupies more than one half of the area, break off the outer end and rewind in the barrel. When the correct area is determined the hook is affixed. A spring of the proper length contains from eleven to thirteen coils. More than the required number of coils only tends to increase friction and shorten the number of hours of running of the watch.

The Dial Train

The cannon pinion, minute wheel, minute pinion, and hour wheel make up the dial train. Referring to Figure 4, the

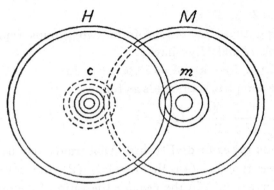

Figure 4.   Dial train.

dial train is arranged as follows. The cannon pinion, *c*, gears into the minute wheel, *M*. The minute pinion, *m*, to which the minute wheel is attached, gears into the hour wheel, *H*. This latter wheel fits freely over the cannon pinion. The minute hand, of course, makes 12 turns to one of the hour hand. The formula for the dial train, therefore, reads as follows:

$$\frac{HM}{cm} = 12$$

Let us suppose we wish to determine the number of teeth of wheels and the number of leaves of pinions of a new dial train. We shall decide on 12 leaves for the cannon pinion, *c*, and 10 leaves for the minute pinion, *m*. Letting *H* indicate the hour wheel and *M* the minute wheel, the equation reads:

$$\frac{HM}{cm} = \frac{HM}{12 \times 10} = 12$$

$HM = 12 \times 12 \times 10 ; HM = 1,440$

Factoring in the manner as heretofore explained, we find that:

$HM = 2^5 \times 3^2 \times 5$

Combining these factors to form two groups representing the wheels *H* and *M* we have:

$H = 2^3 \times 5 = 40 ; M = 2^2 \times 3^2 = 36$

Thus the complete train reads as follows:

$$\frac{HM}{cm} = \frac{40 \times 36}{12 \times 10} = 12$$

Various types of dial trains. Dial trains may be grouped into three types: (1) the regular, (2) the reverse, and (3) the irregular. In the *regular* the ratio of cannon pinion to minute wheel is 3 to 1 and the ratio of the minute pinion to the hour wheel is 4 to 1.

$$\frac{M}{c} = \frac{36}{12} = 3 ; \quad \frac{H}{m} = \frac{40}{10} = 4$$

In the *reverse* the ratio of the cannon pinion to minute wheel is 4 to 1 and the ratio of the minute pinion to hour wheel is 3 to 1.

$$\frac{M}{c} = \frac{32}{8} = 4 ; \quad \frac{H}{m} = \frac{24}{8} = 3$$

The *irregular* does not belong to either of the above types, as shown by the following example:

$$\frac{HM}{cm} = \frac{35 \times 48}{14 \times 10} = \frac{48 \times 26}{13 \times 8} = \frac{32 \times 45}{12 \times 10} = 12$$

Thus the dial train may be formed by working out various combinations, the only requirement being that the combined ratios equal 12. The most used, however, is the 3 to 1— 4 to 1 type referred to as the regular.

Calculating the teeth and leaves of missing mobiles. Let us suppose that the cannon pinion is missing from the following train in which c represents the cannon pinion:

$$\frac{54 \times 32}{c \times 12} = 12$$

$$\frac{144}{c} = 12$$

$$144 = 12c$$

$$12c = 144$$

$$c = 12 \quad \text{leaves of the cannon pinion.}$$

We now wish to find the number of teeth of a missing hour wheel in which H represents the wheel.

$$\frac{H \times 25}{10 \times 10} = 12$$

$$\frac{H}{4} = 12$$

$$H = 48 \text{ teeth of the hour wheel.}$$

Let us suppose that a complete minute wheel and pinion are missing in which M is the wheel and m is the pinion.

$$\frac{48 \times M}{14 \times m} = 12$$

$$\frac{24 M}{7 m} = 12$$

$$\frac{M}{m} = \frac{12 \times 7}{24} = \frac{7}{2} = \frac{3\frac{1}{2}}{1}$$

The result shows that the minute wheel must have $3\frac{1}{2}$ times as many teeth as the minute pinion has leaves. Thus

$$\frac{M}{m} = \frac{28}{8} = \frac{35}{10} = \frac{42}{12} = \frac{49}{14}$$

Any of the above solutions may be used as the following equations will show.

$$\frac{48 \times 28}{14 \times 8} = \frac{48 \times 35}{14 \times 10} = \frac{48 \times 42}{14 \times 12} = \frac{48 \times 49}{14 \times 14} = 12$$

Problems

1. What is meant by train?
2. How many trains has the ordinary watch? Name them.
3. Name the wheels of the average main train.
4. How many turns does the escape wheel make to one of the center wheel in an 18,000-beats-per-hour train? How many turns in a 19,800-beats-per-hour-train?
5. What are the arguments in favor of the fast trains for very small wrist watches?
6. What portion of the space between the barrel and the arbor should the mainspring occupy?
7. What is the correct thickness of the mainspring if the barrel has 80 teeth with an inside diameter of 13 millimeters and the center pinion has 10 leaves?
8. Name the parts of the dial train.
9. How many turns does the hour wheel make in 12 hours?
10. Name the various types of dial trains. Explain their difference.

CHAPTER TWO

Gearing

Terminology

GEARING CONSTITUTES a system of wheels and pinions whose circumferences are covered with teeth so that the teeth of the wheel act upon the leaves of a pinion. The function is in reality as a system of levers in which a longer lever presses on a short one until one lever ceases to press and another lever comes into action.

Gearing is a rather technical subject and it is well first to study Figure 5. The terms given in the illustration are defined as follows:

Pitch circle: a circle concentric with the circumference of a toothed wheel and cutting its teeth at such a distance from their points as to touch the corresponding circle of the pinion working with it, and having with that circle a common velocity, as in a rolling contact.

Pitch diameter: the diameter of the pitch circle.

Full diameter: the diameter from point to point of the teeth.

Distance of centers: the distance measured on a straight line from center to center between the wheel and pinion.

Line of centers: a line drawn from center to center of any wheel and pinion.

Circular pitch: the pitch circle divided into as many spaces as there are teeth on the wheel or pinion.

Diametrical pitch: the diameter of the pitch circle divided into as many spaces as there are teeth on wheel or pinica.

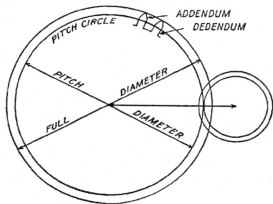

Figure 5.

Addendum: the portion of the tooth, either of wheel or pinion, outside of the pitch circle.

Dedendum: the portion of the tooth of either wheel or pinion inside of the pitch circle.

Driver: the mobile that forces the other along.

Driven: the mobile that is being forced along by the driver.

Principles of Gearing

The addenda. In Figure 6 is shown a portion of a circle, *A,* representing the pitch circle of a wheel. Rolling on this portion of a circle is another circle, *B,* the diameter of which

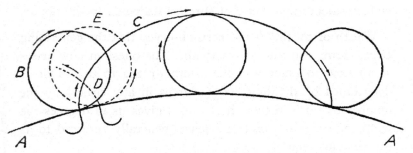

Figure 6.   Formation of the epicycloidal curve.

equals half the pitch diameter of the pinion.   If a pencil point were fixed at the lowest point of the circumference of the smaller circle (the generating circle) and then rolled on the larger circle without slipping, a curve would be traced along the path of the line *C* in the direction of the arrow. The curve thus formed is called the epicycloid and determines the shape of the addenda of the wheel teeth.

The dedenda.   The dedenda of the pinion leaves is formed by the same generating circle but not in the same manner. The smallet circle is rolled inside and along the pitch circle of the pinion.   However, instead of a curved line a radial line is formed as shown by the line *A* in Figure 7.   A circle rolling within a circle is called a hypocycloid and determines the shape of the dedenda of the pinion leaves.   Thus when a wheel and pinion are made in conformance with the above principles of de-

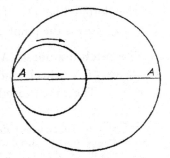

Figure 7.

sign, a smooth and constant force is delivered to the pinion.

Width of tooth. It has been observed that the generating circle forms one side of the tooth. The question now arises as to how to determine the width of the tooth. This is determined by dividing 360 (degrees in any circle) by the number of teeth in the wheel. This gives us in degrees the width of one tooth and one space, generally referred to as the circular pitch.

Thus $\dfrac{360}{80 \text{ teeth}} = 4.5$ degrees circular pitch.

The width of the tooth is equal to one half of the circular pitch; the other half is, of course, equal to the space

Therefore $\dfrac{4\,5 \text{ degrees}}{2} = 2.25$

of which 2.25 degrees is the width of the tooth and 2 25 degrees the width of the space.

Now, by placing the generating circle, *E*, Figure 6, with the pencil point directly below and 2 25 degrees to the right of curve *C*, it will be in position to trace out the other side of the tooth by simply rolling the circle to the left as shown by the dotted line *D* The intersection of the two curves, *C* and *D*, forms the point of the tooth

The pitch diameter. We now wish to determine the pitch diameter of a wheel and pinion, the center distance being known.* The first procedure is to determine the diametrical

---

* The center distance is determined by means of a depthing tool, an instrument with adjustable male centers that can be adjusted to the holes in the plate and conveniently measured with a micrometer or Boley gauge

pitch, the formula for which reads as follows:

$$\frac{\text{center distance} \times 2}{\text{teeth of wheel} + \text{leaves of pinion}} = \text{diametrical pitch.}$$

The diametrical pitch is now multiplied by the number of teeth in the wheel in order to determine the pitch diameter of the wheel, and in like manner the diametrical pitch is multiplied by the number of leaves in the pinion to determine the pitch diameter of the pinion.

For example, the center distance is 8 5 millimeters, the wheel has 80 teeth; the pinion has 10 leaves. Substituting the numerical values for the above formula, we have:

$$\frac{8.5 \times 2}{80 + 10} = .1888 \text{ diametrical pitch.}$$

Continuing the problem we find that:

1888 × 80 = 15.104 mm. pitch diameter of the wheel.

.1888 × 10 = 1.888 mm pitch diameter of the pinion.

$$Proof: \frac{15\ 104 + 1.888}{2} = 8.496 \text{ mm., the distance between}$$

centers.

The full diameter. The height of the addenda is a varying quantity depending on the ratio of the wheel to the pinion, but the production of theoretically correct gears or even knowing when they exist is not possible with the equipment available to the practising horologist The usual practice is to add 2.5 diametrical pitches to the pitch diameter of the wheel and 1.25 to the pitch diameter of the pinion.* Experi-

---

* There is one exception to the above statement. For the dial train where the pinions drive the wheels and the wheels drive the pinions, as in the case of setting the watch to time, the addenda is figured as 2 for both wheels and pinions.

ence has shown that the above figures are best for all practical purposes.

We found that the wheel has for its pitch diameter 15.104 millimeters and the pinion 1.888 millimeters. The diametrical pitch multiplied by 2.5 gives us the height of the addenda for the wheel:

.1888 × 2.5 = .47

Adding this to the pitch diameter of the wheel, we have:

15.104 + .47 = 15 57 mm. full diameter of the wheel.

Now, figuring the pinion we have:

.1888 × 1.25 = .236

1.888 + .236 = 2.12 mm. full diameter of the pinion.

We may, however, figure the full diameters with a lot less work by adding 2.5 or 1.25 (addenda) to the number of the teeth or leaves. For example:

(80 + 2 5) .1888 = 15 57 mm. full diameter of the wheel.

(10 + 1.25) .1888 = 2.12 mm. full diameter of the pinion.

Circular pitch. It will be noted that the definition for circular pitch reads somewhat like the definition for diametrical pitch. The difference is: circular pitch is the division of the circumference of a circle (the pitch circle), whereas the diametrical pitch is the division of the diameter of a circle (the pitch diameter) In both cases the number of teeth or leaves is the divisor

We must know the actual width of tooth and space in order to select a cutter to make a wheel. Herein lies the importance of calculating the circular pitch. To attain this we make use of the following formula:

$$\frac{\text{pitch diameter} \times 3.1416}{\text{teeth or leaves}} = \text{one circular pitch}$$

Substituting the numerical values:

$$\frac{15.1 \times 3\,1416}{80} = .592 \text{ mm. circular pitch}$$

The proportion of tooth or leaf to space is usually:

for the wheels: one half of the circular pitch

for the pinions, 10 leaves or less: one third of the circular pitch.

for the pinions, 12 leaves or more · two fifths of the circular pitch.

Now, continuing with the above example to determine the width of the tooth of the wheel and the leaf of the pinion, we find that

$$\frac{.592}{2} = .296 \text{ mm., the width of the tooth, and}$$

$$\frac{.592}{3} = .197 \text{ mm., the width of the leaf.}$$

Problems

1. What is the epicycloid? the hypocycloid?
2. Define diametrical pitch
3. Calculate the diametrical pitch for the following:

center distance—7 5 millimeters

wheel—75 teeth.

pinion—10 leaves.

4. Calculate the pitch diameter for the above wheel and pinion. Calculate the full diameters
5. Define circular pitch
6. Calculate the circular pitch, using the specifications given in Problem 3.

CHAPTER THREE

The Lever Escapement

TIME AND EXPERIENCE have demonstrated the superiority of the lever escapement over all other types for portable timepieces. In fact, the several other types have now become obsolete. Since its introduction by Thomas Mudge in 1750 the lever escapement has been the object of much experimentation and study. It finally was developed into the state of perfection we see it today only after a number of unique and fantastic variations were tried and discarded.

Terminology

The several parts of the escapement are defined as follows:

ESCAPE WHEEL

The escape wheel is that part of an escapement that delivers impulse to the balance through the medium of a pallet fork.

Ratchet-tooth wheel: the name given to the English type escape wheel, which has pointed teeth.

Club-tooth wheel: that type of escape wheel which has a lifting face at the end of the teeth. *Impulse face:* the lifting plane of a club-tooth wheel. *Locking face:* the slanting face of the teeth on which the pallets lock. *Toe:* the intersection of the locking face and the impulse face of a club tooth.

Heel. the intersection of the impulse face and the letting-off corner of a club tooth.

PALLET FORK

The pallet fork is that part of an escapement that, by means of pallet jewels, receives impulse from the escape wheel and delivers impulse to the balance.

Pallets: the name given to the metal body to which the lever is attached. The term includes the pallet jewels.

Lever: a metal piece attached to the pallets that carries impulse to the balance. The *fork* occupies the extreme end of the lever.

Fork slot: a notch cut into the fork for the reception of the roller jewel.

Horns: the circular sides of the fork that lead to the fork slot.

Receiving pallet: that pallet stone over which a tooth of the escape wheel slides in order to enter between the pallet stones.

Discharging pallet: that pallet stone over which a tooth of the escape wheel slides in order to leave from between the pallets. *Impulse face:* the lifting plane of the pallet stone. *Letting-off corner:* the extreme end of the impulse face of a pallet stone where the tooth of the escape wheel lets off *Locking face:* the face of a pallet stone on which a tooth locks.

ROLLER TABLE

The roller table is the circular disk that carries the roller jewel.

Crescent: a circular notch in the edge of the roller table for the reception of the guard pin or finger.

Single roller: a roller action comprising a single metal disk.

Double roller: a roller action comprising two metal disks, the larger disk carrying the roller jewel and a smaller disk in which a crescent is cut.

Roller jewel or **jewel pin:** a flattened jewel that is inserted in the roller table.

BANKING PINS

Banking pins are pins that arrest or limit the angular motion of the lever.

Equidistant, Circular and Semitangental Pallets

There are three types of pallet arrangements used in the lever escapement: the equidistant, the circular and the semitangental.

Equidistant pallets. In the equidistant the locking faces of the pallets are an equal distance from the pallet center,

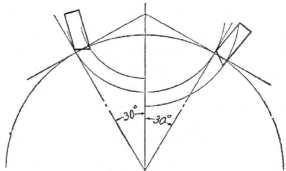

Figure 8.   Equidistant pallets.

as shown in Figure 8. As a result the lifting action on the discharging pallet takes place too far from the point of tangency, necessitating the need for a greater lifting angle on that stone. Although the unlocking is performed under favorable conditions, the lifting action is not, being unequal in its distribution and unequal also as to the pressure of the tooth on the pallets. This escapement calls for exceptional accuracy in its construction.

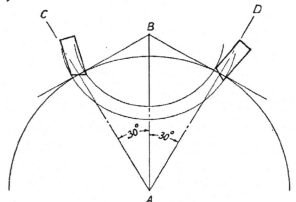

Figure 9.   Circular pallets.

Circular pallets. Circular pallets have the central portion of the pallets' lifting faces an equal distance from the pallet center as shown by the lines *CA* and *DA* in Figure 9. One half of the width of the pallets is placed on each side of these lines, which requires that the locking faces stand at an unequal distance from the pallet center, causing an unequal and increased unlocking resistance. However, the action of lift is more favorable.

Semitangental pallets. Setting on the locking is a common fault in small wrist watches; hence a light lock is

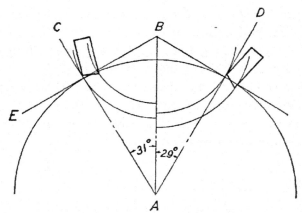

Figure 10.   Semitangental pallets.

essential to good performance.   With regard to this factor
the semitangental escapement, a development of recent years,
has found favor with many manufacturers because it lessens
the resistance to unlocking, a natural fault with the circular,
and at the same time minimizes the lifting error of the
equidistant.   Figure 10 shows the semitangental escapement.
It will be observed that the unlocking on the receiving pallet
takes place on the tangent *EB* at the intersection of *CA*.
A slightly increased center distance results, since the line
CA is placed 31 degrees to the left of the center line *BA*.
The action of the discharging pallet is similar to that of an
escapement with circular pallets.   The designers claim that
the unlocking and lifting actions are more nearly equally
divided than any escapement that has yet been conceived.

Number of Teeth in Escape Wheel

Although nearly all watches have an escape wheel of 15
teeth we may make them with 12, 14, 16, or practically any

number in this range. The first lever escapement as made by Thomas Mudge had an escape wheel of 20 teeth. The larger numbers result in a rather clumsy action and are therefore not satisfactory. Escapements using a wheel of 12 or 14 teeth are used today in some wrist watches and have certain advantages. For example, there is more clearance between the pallet arm and the escape wheel. The smaller number of teeth permit the use of wider pallet jewels and a wider lifting plane for the teeth. Also the actual measurement of 1½ degrees of locking is greater because of the increased distance between the locking corners of the pallets and the pallet center.

Wheel and Pallet Action

The lever escapement has two distinct and separate functions: (1) the action of the wheel and pallets and (2) that of the fork and roller These functions we shall now consider. The first, which has to do with the wheel and pallets, is divided into three actions. They are:

1 the locking
2 the draw
3 impulse or lift

The locking. The locking is the overlapping of a tooth on a pallet when the lever rests against the bank. This locking is necessary for the reason that if one tooth lets off a pallet and another tooth falls directly on the impulse face of the opposite pallet, there is a recoil of the lever toward the balance, causing a frictional contact between the guard pin and roller table. Contact in this manner would immediately stop the watch To avoid this a certain amount of lock is necessary. However, it should be as little as possible consistent with the proper safety in action.

The draw. In portable timepieces the lock in itself is not sufficient to insure safety in action. It is necessary to create an action whereby the pallets are drawn into the wheel This is effected by inclining the locking faces of the pallets to the right of the lines CA and DA as shown in Figure 10 This slanting should be as little as possible, yet enough to overcome the friction of the tooth on the surface of the pallets, for it can readily be seen that the combined action of lock and draw makes a resistance to the motion of the balance and has an important relationship to the position and isochronal rating of a watch.

It is generally conceded that 12 degrees draw on each pallet is satisfactory. However, because of the circular motion of the pallets the draw is changing continually, being strongest on the receiving pallet at the point of unlocking, whereas on the discharging pallet it is weakest at the point of unlocking. The nature of this action leads one to assume that a greater angle for draw should be given to the receiving pallet; in fact, we find some authorities designing the escapement with 13 to 15 degrees draw on the receiving pallet. This would make the draw more nearly equal at the point of banking where it is most needed

The lift. In well-designed escapements of the club-tooth variety the actual lift is 8½ degrees, being divided between tooth and pallets in varying proportions Adding 1½ degrees for the lock, the total angular motion of the lever becomes 10 degrees.

Width of pallet and tooth. It will be observed that a

wide pallet requires a narrow tooth ; likewise a narrow pallet should be associated with a wide tooth if the drop* is to be kept to the minimum. In this connection several pallet and tooth combinations are listed below :

CIRCULAR PALLETS

	PALLET			TOOTH	
	Lift	*Width*	*Lift*	*Width*	
1	6 degrees	7 degrees	2½ degrees	3½ degrees	
2	5¼ "	6¼ "	3¼ "	4¼ "	
3	5 "	6 "	3½ "	4½ "	
4	4 "	5 "	4½ "	5½ "	

EQUIDISTANT PALLETS

	Lift	*Width*	*Lift*	*Width*	
5	6 degrees	7 degrees	2½ degrees	3½ degrees	
6	5½ "	6 "	3 "	4½ "	
7	5½ "	5¾ "	3 "	4¼ "	

Attention should be given to this fact: in the equidistant pallets the lift on the tooth should be less than the lift on the pallets.   Circular and equidistant pallets are not always interchangeable.   However, there are exceptions, as in the case of Number *1* and Number *5*, which are alike and have been interchanged by Grossman. Number *4* is suitable only for circular pallets, especially so since the narrow pallets perform the act of locking nearer to the lines *CA* and *DA,* as shown in Figure 9. Numbers *5* and *6* would be suitable also for the semitangental escapement

---

Drop is a term used to indicate the free motion of the escape wheel after one tooth lets off a pallet and another tooth locks on the opposite pallet This factor is of more concern in practical benchwork and is treated fully in Part II, Chapter Six

The Fork and Roller Action

Unlocking and impulse actions. The relation between the fork and roller jewel as a mechanical action may be divided into two distinct and separate functions: (1) the unlocking of the pallets and (2) the impulse to the balance. One action is the reverse of the other. The unlocking action takes place as a result of power derived from the balance and spring, while the impulse to the balance receives its energy from the force delivered to the escape wheel by means of the main spring and the train. In the unlocking action, a short lever (roller-jewel radius) acts on a longer one (the lever fork). A short roller-jewel radius must be associated with a long lever which involves a large angle of contact as shown by the angle *ABC* in Figure 11. On the other hand, a long roller-jewel radius must be associated with a short lever which results in a small angle of contact as shown by the angle *ABC* in Figure 12. In other words, the shorter the roller-jewel radius the larger is the angle of contact, and the smaller the angle of contact the longer is the roller-jewel radius.

A 4-to-1 roller action. In Figure 11 the relation of the roller jewel to the fork slot is 4 to 1; that is, the lever moves 10 degrees and the roller jewel remains in contact with the fork slot for a space of 40 degrees. The action of unlocking begins quite some distance from the line of centers because of the short roller-jewel radius. However, a short roller-jewel radius results in a much safer action and an easier unlocking of the pallets.

A 3-to-1 roller action. In Figure 12 the relation of the roller jewel to the fork slot is 3 to 1. Although the unlocking action is more difficult, the impulse to the balance is more energetic when it does occur. The 30-degree contact of the roller jewel with the fork slot is in accord with the theory that the lever should be as highly detached as possible for finer results in timing.

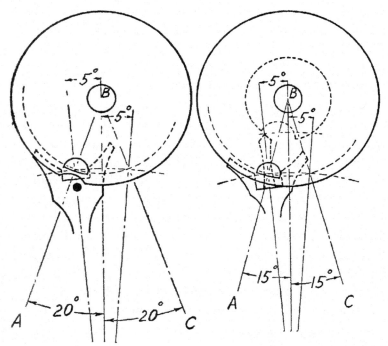

Figure 11. Fork and roller action—single roller.   Figure 12. Fork and roller action—double roller.

The more delicate safety action of a long roller-jewel radius is not a problem in high-grade watches, for in such work we naturally expect a mechanical action that is more exact in its function. It follows, therefore, that a long roller-jewel radius which involves a small angle of contact is one of the important factors to be considered in fine escapement design   Of course, in the cheaper work and in small wrist watches it is not always practical.

A wide roller jewel. The wide roller jewel results in a particularly satisfactory action of unlocking by taking place near the line of centers. However, the impulse to the balance is not so favorable. A wide roller jewel is inseparable from a long roller-jewel radius, for such a principle of design results in a very delicate action. A wide roller jewel makes the safety action much less delicate.

A narrow roller jewel. A wide roller jewel, if associated with a short roller-jewel radius, causes an unfavorable impulse to the balance too far from the line of centers, and the "uphill" circular path of the roller jewel along the side of the fork slot during the impulse to the balance results in considerable friction. Also, on account of the greater angle at which the roller jewel stands to the slot when the impulse takes place, the drop of the fork against the jewel will amount to more than its shake in the slot, if measured when standing on the line of centers. Thus a narrow roller jewel is better adapted for a short roller-jewel radius, and should always be associated with a single-roller escapement.

Single-roller escapement. In the single-roller escapement, Figure 11, it is required that the roller table be as small as possible to preserve the safety action. Furthermore, friction between the guard pin and the circumference of the roller table would be considerably increased on a table roller that was larger than necessary. It is difficult to reduce the angular motion of the lever to less than 10 degrees, and any relation of fork to roller jewel less than a $3\frac{1}{2}$ to 1 is not practical.

Double-roller escapement. We have learned that in order to favor the impulse to the balance we require a long roller-jewel radius, and for the safety action a short radius. This is the reason for the passing of the single-roller escapement in favor of the double-roller type, Figure 12, for in the latter type we have two rollers, one for each action

The size of the safety roller is of no great importance. For the sake of soundness in action its radius should not be less than one half the radius of the roller jewel. The smaller the safety roller the sooner will the crescent approach the guard finger; and, likewise, the longer the roller-jewel radius the later will the roller jewel enter the fork slot. It follows, therefore, that the greater the difference between the respective radii of the roller jewel and the safety roller the longer must be the horns of the fork. The width of the roller jewel also plays a part in the length of the horns, for with any increase in the width of the jewel, the horns may be made proportionately shorter.

The crescent. The circular notch in the roller is called the *crescent* and should be wide and deep enough so that it will be impossible for the guard finger to touch any part of it. If made too wide, longer horns on the fork would be required to preserve the safety action

The width of the crescent in the double-roller escapement is greater than in the single-roller type, for the reason that the guard finger, due to its increased length, has a larger space to cover for its safety action, or, stating the function in another way: it could be said that the velocity of the guard finger has increased, whereas the velocity of the safety roller has decreased.

Problems

1. How do the equidistant pallets differ from the circular pallets?
2. Compare the above with the semi-tangental escapement.
3. What is meant by locking?
4. Define draw. How does draw differ on the receiving pallet as compared with the draw on the discharging pallet?
5. How many degrees are generally intended for the lifting action?
6. Explain the difference between a 4 to 1 and 3 to 1 roller action.
7. Which of the above actions is preferred? Why?
8. Describe the single and double escapements State the advantages and disadvantages of each type.
9. What is the name of the small roller that makes up the double-roller escapement?
10. What is the purpose of the crescent?

CHAPTER FOUR

The Controlling Mechanism

T HE BALANCE and balance spring are the most vital parts of a watch and may be properly called the controlling mechanism. Years ago the principal difficulty in maintaining accurate time was the temperature error, since the compensating balance was unknown prior to 1769. Often the error was as much as four or five minutes in twenty-four hours. The variation is due to three conditions: (1) the expansion and contraction of the metal in the balance, (2) changes in the length of the balance spring, and (3) variation of the elastic force of the spring. The variation of the elastic force of the spring is the most important factor; in fact, Ferdinand Berthoud has estimated that 82 per cent of the error is due to the variation of the elastic force.

Experimental demonstration. A simple experiment to prove the correctness of the above statement may be tried

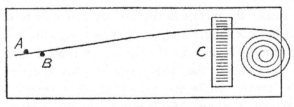

Figure 13.

if desired. The materials needed are a sheet of brass about 4 or 5 inches long and 2 inches wide, a piece of brass wire, and an old mainspring. Drill two holes, *A* and *B*, Figure 13, about ¼ inch apart and insert two brass pins and rivet securely. Straighten the outer portion of the mainspring and place the end between the pins, the extreme end being placed under pin *A* and over pin *B*, while the coiled portion passes beyond the index *C*. The coil beyond the index will serve as a weight. Now, with the aid of an alcohol lamp and blowpipe heat the brass plate. It will be observed that the spring, after becoming heated slightly, has deflected noticeably, as may be seen by noting the position of the spring on the index. Upon cooling it will return to its original position.

Temperature Error of the Balance and Balance Spring

The compensating balance. The compensating balance, or bimetallic balance, as it is sometimes called, Figure 14, was designed to overcome the errors resulting from the use of the solid balance. This balance is constructed by brazing together brass and steel for the rim of the balance. The brass is on the outside and constitutes about three fifths of the total thickness.

Heat causes the metals in the balance assembly to expand; the arms become longer and, as the brass expands more than the steel, the loose ends of the rim curve inward toward the center. Cold causes the loose ends to move outward away from the center, while the arms become shorter. This is clearly shown in Figure 15. It will be further observed that the loose ends remain reasonably circular during temperature

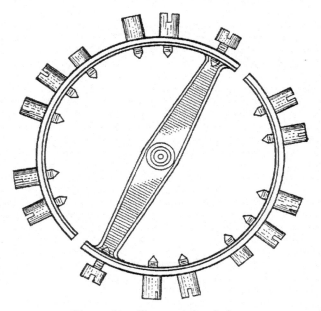

Figure 14.   Compensating balance.

changes, but the radii of the curves change, their centers being at the balance center O for the normal temperature and shifting along the arms AA for the high and low temperatures. However, the points BB, about 60 degrees from the arms, remain at a fixed distance from the balance center, and it is at these points that alterations for the purpose of timing should be made.

Middle-temperature error. It is evident from the above analysis that we can adjust the balance screws in such a manner as to compensate for the expansion and contraction of the balance alone and maintain a constant mean diameter. This, however, would not take care of the lengthening and shortening of the balance spring nor for the changes in the

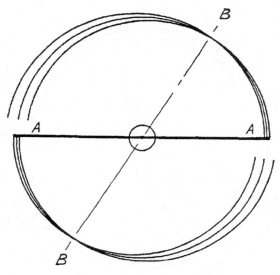

Figure 15.

elastic force. To compensate for the effects of temperature on the spring, it is necessary to add extra weight to the loose ends of the rim. This results in a temperature error, between the extremes of heat and cold, known as the *middle-temperature error* due to the fact that the balance does not compensate equally for changes in the elastic force and for changes in the length of the spring. This is shown by insufficient compensation (weights not moving in near enough toward the center of the balance) in the higher temperatures; and too great a compensation (weights moving too far away from the center) in the lower temperatures. The result is a higher rate in the normal temperature, usually from two to six seconds in twenty-four hours, depending on the grade of the watch.

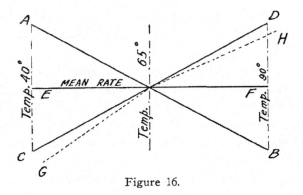

Figure 16.

This factor is clearly shown in Figure 16. The line *AB* indicates the uniform loss in the rate due to a rising temperature on the balance spring only. To exactly offset this rate by some means of compensating the error, we must produce the opposite effect indicated by the line *CD*. The theoretical results would be a constant mean rate along the line *EF*.

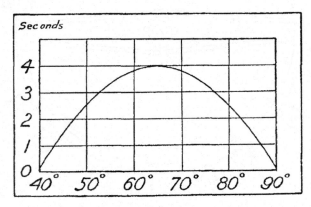

Figure 17.   Middle-temperature error.

However, since the actual compensating effect of the balance alone lies along the dotted line *GH*, the actual rate is similar to that shown in Figure 17.

There is no way of rectifying this condition except to use a nickle-steel alloy called *Invar*, the perfection of which has been realized only in recent years. This remarkable metal expands and contracts only a very little for changes in temperature, and in using it instead of the ordinary steel the middle-temperature error is considerably reduced.

Still more recently another type of alloy made of iron, nickle-chromium, and tungsten and known as *Elinvar* has

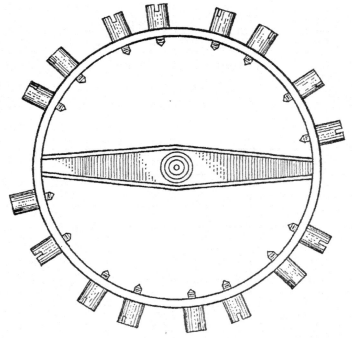

Figure 18. Solid balance.

been developed for the use of balance springs. Elinvar maintains a constant elasticity and is, therefore, used in connection with a solid, single-metal balance as shown in Figure 18. The metal has the further advantages of being nonrusting and only slightly subject to magnetism. Also there can be no middle-temperature error.

The Balance Spring

There are two forms of balance springs in general use. These are the flat spring, Figure 19, and the Breguet, Figure 20. The former has the stud fixed to the same plane as the body of the spring, with the result that the vibrations take place in an eccentric manner. The latter, referred to as Breguet, has a portion of the outer coil raised above and over the body of the spring. The original Breguet spring was created by Abraham Louis Breguet (1747-1823), famous French horologist, but the spring by him bore no resemblance

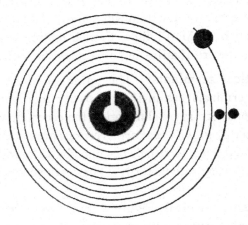

Figure 19. Flat balance spring.

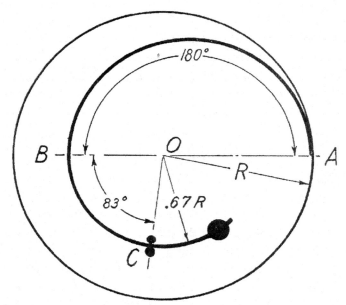

Figure 20. Overcoil balance spring.

to the theoretical terminals as applied to modern watches. The terminals as we now find them are based on the foundation laid down by M. Phillips, French mining engineer, and have placed the art of adjusting on a scientific basis.

Theoretical terminals. The value of the theoretically corrected terminals lies in their capacity to correct position and isochronal errors by eliminating the eccentric wanderings of the center of gravity that are everpresent in the flat spring. The outer and inner terminals designed by L. Lossier perform this function very satisfactorily. These are shown in Figures 20 and 21.

In the outer terminal, Figure 20, note that the overcoil is composed of portions of two circles. The outer coil tends

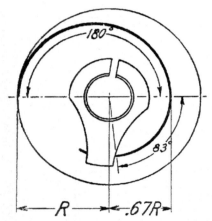

Figure 21. Theoretical inner terminal.

inward at *A* and forms an arc of 180 degrees to *B*, which is planted at a point equal to *.67* of the radius *R*. The overcoil continues for another 83 degrees, the radius of which is *CO*. To this must be added the amount necessary to reach through the stud.

Figure 21 shows the Lossier inner terminal. The elements of the curve are the same as the outer terminal and are clearly shown in the illustration. Although the overcoil is applied to practically all watches today, the theoretically corrected inner terminal is not, its use being confined only to the very finest watches. The reason no doubt lies in the fact that the Lossier inner terminal is difficult to make and harder to adjust and, unless the curve is 100 per cent perfect, it is no better than a true terminal of the ordinary type. Careful poising of the collet is also necessary.

Problems

1. Describe the compensating balance.
2. What is the middle-temperature error?
3. What type of balance springs are used with solid, single-metal balance wheels?
4. How does the Breguet spring differ from the flat spring?
5. What are the advantages of the theoretical terminals?
6. Draw a sketch showing the proportions of the theoretical curves, both outside and inside.

PART II

PRACTICAL REPAIRING

CHAPTER ONE

Train Problems

General observations in gearing. Attention should always be paid to the action of the outgoing tooth, noting that its point is not used and that the incoming tooth takes up its load without drop. The incoming tooth should begin pressing on the pinion leaf as near as possible to the line of centers, allowing for the fact that this is a varying quantity depending on the number of leaves in the pinion. The best possible actions for pinions of ten, eight, and six leaves are shown in Figures 1, 2, and 3. Note that in Figure 1 the action begins on the line of centers, in Figure 2 slightly before the line of centers, and in Figure 3 quite some distance from the line of centers.

Gearing may be found defective with regard to several factors. Below are listed the most common.

Pinion too large
Pinion too small
Depthing too deep
Depthing too shallow

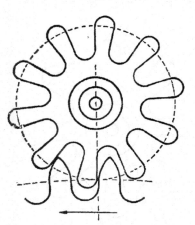

Figure 1. Ten-leaf pinion.

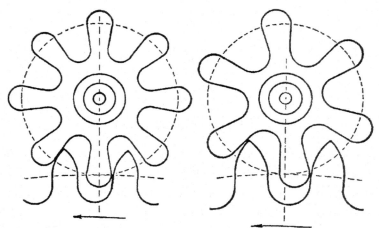

Figure 2. Eight-leaf pinion.　　　Figure 3. Six-leaf pinion.

Let us now examine the errors in the order listed above.

Pinion too large. Referring to Figure 4 it will be observed that the incoming tooth butts into the end of the pinion

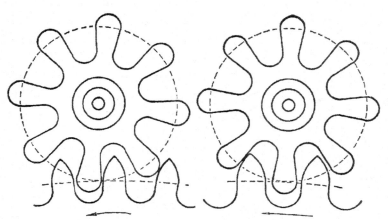

Figure 4. Pinion too large.　　　Figure 5. Pinion too small.

leaf, thereby stopping the watch. If the error is slight the action can be improved by enlarging the wheel, in which case the outgoing tooth will propel its leaf farther, resulting in a sufficient clearance between the incoming leaf and the incoming tooth.

Pinion too small. A pinion too small, Figure 5, results in a waste of power and much noise, since the outgoing tooth propels the leaf even to the point of slipping off before the incoming tooth has started to press on a leaf. Hence, if much too small, the incoming tooth will fall with a click on the leaf. Wear is considerable and an error of this kind should never be allowed to pass without correction. The fitting of a larger pinion is the only satisfactory solution.

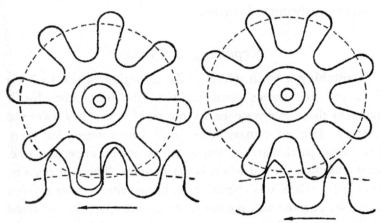

Figure 6. Depthing too deep.   Figure 7. Depthing too shallow.

Depthing too deep. In a depthing too deep, Figure 6, the outgoing tooth continues its action too long, most likely with the point affected by excessive wear and a loss of power.

Depthing too shallow. A shallow depth, Figure 7, is always unsatisfactory Note that the outgoing tooth cannot propel its leaf far enough and the incoming tooth presses on a leaf before the line of centers In a very shallow depth a butting action usually results. Enlarging the wheel sometimes puts the depth in a passable condition.

Worn pinions. If a watch stops in the train and starts with the slightest movement it is well to look at the pinions and see if they are worn. Modern wrist watches frequently use a six-leaf escape pinion, which when well designed gives good service, but has the disadvantage of about 18 degrees engaging in friction. Wear is as a result quite pronounced and in time will cause trouble. Often the fourth wheel can be raised or lowered so that the wheel drives the pinion on the previously unused portion.

Repairing a Train

Stretching a train wheel. The enlarging of train wheels is a job that comes occasionally to the horologist, for it happens that some watches are not right when they leave the factory. It is, of course, better to fit a new wheel, but there are times, particularly if the watch is not an expensive one, that enlarging the old wheel is permissible The fact remains that if the wheel was imperfect to begin with and we make it serve its purpose and the watch runs better, we feel justified in the act.

The staking tool may be used to stretch the wheel It is preferred that we work on the lower side of the wheel, so that the markings made by the flat punch will not be visible when the watch is assembled We first select a hole in the die to loosely fit either the staff of the pinion or the entire pinion as the case may require. The die is so adjusted that the rim of the wheel comes under the punch. It frequently happens that the part of the rim we wish to work on comes over, or partly over, another hole in the die. When this happens we may select a larger hole and plug it with pith. This will hold a staff in position while stretching the rim over a smooth and solid part of the die.

To stretch a wheel we use a flat-face punch of such width as to completely cover the rim including the teeth. Tap the punch gently a succession of blows and at the same time turn the wheel slowly. This stretches the rim satisfactorily and with scarcely any visible punch marks, except where the arms are crossed.

To keep the wheel as nearly round as possible, it is necessary to stretch the arms, as we should not rely on the cutter of the rounding-up tool to bring the wheel circular. Stretching of the arms is done separately—that is, after the enlarging of the rim and teeth—and great care should be exercised so as not to overdo the stretching.

The rounding-up tool. Having finished the stretching we are ready to use the rounding-up tool. First, select one of the brass beds the diameter of which is sufficient to support the wheel and at the same time be perfectly free of the cutter. Next, select a cutter that exactly fits the space between the teeth. Occasionally, we find wheels the teeth of which are too wide. In such cases a wider cutter is required in order to reduce the teeth to a width that will satisfactorily gear into the pinion. Having selected the cutter and placed it in the tool, we center it in line with the guide, a knifelike piece provided for the purpose of making certain that the teeth will be cut perfectly upright. The wheel to be rounded-up is now placed between centers and so adjusted that the wheel turns freely and the rim barely touches the brass bed. Carefully advance the cutter so as to engage it with the wheel. See also that the guide on the cutter is properly centered within the space preceding the one that the cutter occupies Cut the wheel but proceed carefully. It is well to try the wheel frequently in the watch so as to not overdo the correction

Problems

1. How many leaves are required of a pinion so that the action begins on the line of centers?

2. Name four defects that are sometimes found in gearing.

3. If a train is noisy what may be the reason?

4. Why is a shallow depth always unsatisfactory?

5. If a watch stops frequently in the train, what may be the reason?

CHAPTER TWO

Jeweling

THE USE of jewels as bearings for watches is, without question, one of the most important achievements to the attainment of precision timekeeping. Nicholas Facio, an Italian residing in London, successfully applied jewels to watches about the year 1704. The system used by Facio was not the same as employed in making the jeweled bearing of today. Instead of a hole piercing a jewel, a V-shaped depression was ground into the jewel. The pivot was pointed and worked into the depressed jewel in much the same way as in the present-day alarm clock. The Swiss were quick to realize the advantages of jeweling and began experiments which finally resulted in the making of jewels as we find them today.

Bezel-Type Jeweling

Jeweling of the bezel type is a rather difficult task when attempted by the usual hand methods. Yet the lathe attachment intended for such work is practical only when a considerable number of jewels are to be set. We shall, therefore, describe only the hand method—a method which, after the necessary experience, will satisfy the needs for all practical purposes. Few tools are needed. These are a supply of drills, the usual gravers, a jewel graver, Figure 8, and a burnisher, Figure 9.

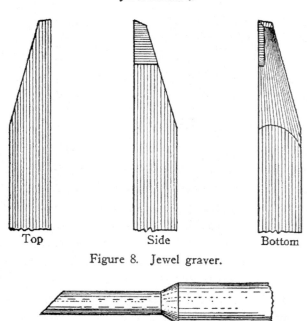

Top   Side   Bottom

Figure 8. Jewel graver.

Figure 9. Jewel burnisher.

The procedure is as follows. Secure in the lathe a piece of four-millimeter brass wire. Face off the end of the wire and turn a small center. Select a drill slightly smaller than the jewel to be used and bore a hole about five millimeters deep. With the jewel graver enlarge the hole slightly to true it up. Next turn a seat to fit the jewel. The depth should be sufficient so that the jewel will lie slightly below the surface of the wire. Next, cut a groove close to the opening for the jewel with a long, pointed graver. The jewel is now to be inserted but should first be moistened with a little oil to keep it from falling out. Now rest the burnisher on the T-rest; thrust the point of the burnisher in the groove,

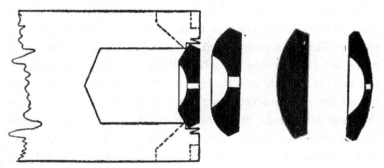

Figure 10.   Figure 11.   Bezel type jewels.

forcing the brass against the jewel, thereby holding the jewel in place. A jewel thus set is perfectly secure and the brass may be faced off level to the jewel if desired. Figure 10 clearly shows the work as described above. The dotted lines in the figure show the manner in which the setting is turned to fit the watch plate. End shake is tried before the wire is cut off. This being satisfactory the wire is cut off, turned to the proper thickness, and stripped out with a sapphire jewel stripper or a highly polished graver. The face is polished by sliding the setting on an agate polishing stone or burnish file previously prepared with a Number-1 buff.

Three styles of bezel-type jewels are used in watches and are shown in Figure 11. The method for setting all styles is the same.

Friction Jeweling

Friction jeweling of watches is a simple and quick method of inserting a jewel in a plate, bridge, or setting by means of friction. Swiss manufacturers started using this system in 1920, and since then more and more manufacturers, both Swiss and American, have adopted this method.

In fitting a friction jewel, the first procedure is to determine the depth the jewel is to be set to give the proper end shake. This is accomplished by using a machine especially made for the purpose, of which there are many varieties on the market. First, rest the pusher on the broken jewel and adjust the metric screw near the top of the machine so that the new jewel may be forced in to the same depth as the broken one had been. Second, push out the broken jewel and ream out the hole with the smallest reamer that will cut away enough metal to give to the plate a clean, straight hole. Third, select the proper jewel, the outside diameter of which is 1/100 of a millimeter larger than the hole in the plate. Remove the burr left by the reamer with the wheel countersinks and push the jewel in place.

Replacing a friction jewel. To replace a jewel in a watch that had a friction jewel in it before, it is necessary only to measure the size of the hole in the plate. This may be done by inserting the reamers or using a special gauge that is available for the purpose. Having determined the hole size, select the jewel required and push it in to the proper depth.

Figure 12. Friction jewels.

Fitting jewel in removable setting. If we wish to fit a jewel in a setting that may be removed from a plate, as in the case of a balance or cap jewel, we need special tools to hold the setting securely while reaming out the hole. There are various types of tools on the market all of which are used in connection with the friction-jeweling machine.

Several types of friction jewels are shown in Figure 12.

Problems

1   What are the tools needed in fitting bezel-type jewels?
2   Name the styles of bezel-type jewels used in watches.
3. How do friction-type jewels differ from bezel-type jewels?
4. How do you determine the depth a friction-type jewel is to be set?

CHAPTER THREE

Making a Balance Staff

MANY HOROLOGISTS consider the making of a balance staff a difficult task. We find workmen doing almost anything to a watch to avoid the necessity of making a staff. Balance bridges are bent up or down. Unsightly graver marks are found on plates and bridges. The balance arms are sometimes bent out of line in an attempt to permit the balance to clear the various parts, and pivots are often ground too short. However, the making of a staff is not difficult if the repairman would go about learning the art the same as with any other performance requiring skill. No one ever learned to play a musical instrument in a few lessons or ever became an expert engraver in a few months.

Preliminary Notes on Staff Making

Gravers for turning staffs. Three gravers of the styles shown in Figure 13 are needed for staff work. *A* is for general use, suitable also for square shoulders and the cylindrical portion of cone pivots. *B* has a rounded point for turning the cone portion of the cone pivot. *C* has the point flattened and is used for turning the lower end of the staff prior to cutting it off.

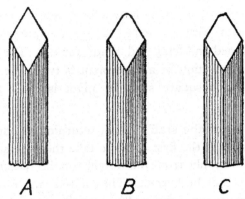

Figure 13.   Gravers for turning balance staff.

Sharpening the gravers.   Sharpening the gravers does not seem to be given the attention by the average horologist that it should. We have seen workmen trying to cut a square shoulder pivot with a graver having a point like a wire nail. Naturally their work was unsuccessful, yet these workmen did not reflect on the fact that possibly the graver was at fault. The graver must have a sharp point. Even the best gravers cannot retain a keen edge very long while cutting tempered steel. Therefore keep a sharpening stone handy and make frequent use of it. Some workmen use an emory or carborundum wheel to grind gravers. This should never be done, as the point of the graver is frequently softened and this point is the most important part. Instead we use two stones, a soft Arkansas stone and a hard Arkansas stone. The soft stone is for rapid cutting and the hard stone is for the final finishing. After grinding the face, slide the sides on the stone so as to produce a flat and smooth cutting surface.

Making pivots for practice.   The beginner should practice making square shoulder and cone pivots before attempting the making of a staff. It will be found that the larger pieces of pivot wire are excellent for the purpose, as the wire is hardened and tempered, ready for use. The length of the cylindrical portion of a cone pivot is twice the diameter. The length of a square shoulder pivot is three times the diameter.

Measuring for the staff. Now, returning to our problem of making a staff, the first act is to take the necessary measurements, preferably from the watch, for the reason that the old staff may not be correct. The well-known Boley gauge serves the purpose very well, since it reads both ways, between the calipers and from the end of the foot. See that the balance bridge lies flat with the lower plate. Now remove the cap jewels. Make certain that the hole jewels are securely pushed in place. For the full length of the staff *A,* Figure 14, measure from the side of the lower hole jewel to

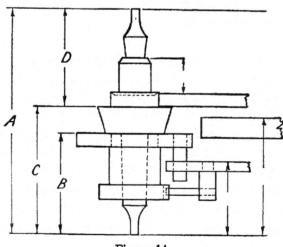

Figure 14.

the side of the upper hole jewel. The height of the seat for the roller table B is found by measuring the distance from the side of the lower hole jewel to the top of the lever, adding enough for clearance and the thickness of the roller table. In like manner the distance for the balance seat C is measured from the side of the lower hole jewel to the top of the pallet bridge, adding for the necessary clearance. The length of the upper end of the staff D is found by subtracting the length of the lower end to balance seat C from the full length A.

Preparing the steel. Preparing the steel wire for the staff is next in order. Select a piece of steel, the diameter of which will be a little larger than the largest part of the staff when finished. Heat over a gas flame to a cherry red and plunge quickly into water. This should be done in a rather dark place so as to see better the degree of heat, for if the light is too bright, one is apt to overheat the steel and thereby ruin it.

The wire is now too hard to turn and we must therefore draw the temper. The wire must be made white in order to blue it. This is done in the lathe by holding a piece of fine emory paper against the wire.

The tempering is done by drawing the wire through the flame of an alcohol lamp; or, better still, lay the wire on a curved sheet of copper, keeping the wire rolling while being held above the lamp. A full blue color is satisfactory for staffs.

Turning the staff. Tighten the wire securely in the lathe, having extended the wire from the chuck sufficiently to include the full length of the staff and about two millimeters

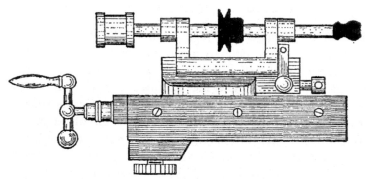

Figure 15. Pivot polisher.

additional. With the hand graver turn the upper end—first turning the balance seat to length from the end and almost to size, say .05 of a millimeter of the finished diameter. Next turn the collet axis, followed by turning the remaining end nearly to the size of the hole in the roller table.

Turning a conical pivot. Turn the cylindrical portion of the pivot almost to size. Next, using the graver with the point slightly rounded, turn the cone, bringing it down to meet the cylindrical portion of the pivot. This is followed by cutting the slope between the collet axis and the cone of the pivot. The turning of the upper end of the staff is now completed and we are ready for the pivot polisher and the preparation of the grinding mediums.

The pivot polisher. The pivot polisher, Figure 15, is a very neat little instrument for grinding and polishing. The superiority of the instrument over any hand method is unquestionable; it does the work in a factory-like manner and polishes the pivot most beautifully. It is to be regretted that the pivot polisher is not more generally used.

However, the successful use of the pivot polisher depends on the proper preparation of the laps and we shall digress for a moment to consider the method by which they are made—how to keep them in good condition, and their various uses. We need laps of cast iron, bell metal, and boxwood, and the material may be purchased from hardware stores and material houses.

Cast-iron and bell-metal laps.   Laps made of cast iron and bell metal are used principally for grinding. The material may be purchased in rods of various diameters. For most needs of the horologists, rods of about ⅝ inch in diameter will suffice. Having selected the materail, saw off a piece about ½ inch long and bore a hole in it of such size that a reamer of the required taper may be used to enlarge the hole. The hole is reamed out with a reamer of the same taper as the taper chuck shown in Figure 16. The blank is placed in the taper chuck for turning with the slide rest. Laps of various shapes are needed. Those most used are shown in Figure 17.

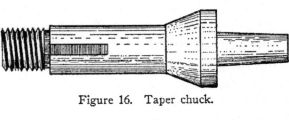

Figure 16.   Taper chuck.

Figure 17.   Laps for pivot polisher.

Having turned the laps, the face and side must be filed to enable the lap to hold the grinding or polishing medium. Filing, it is admitted, has a tendency to destroy its truth, yet this is necessary in order to do good work. Experience has shown that it is possible to file a lap many times and still run practically true. File the lap by laying it face down on a Number 4 or 5 file. Holding the lap between the thumb and fingers, slide the lap along the cutting teeth of the file about an inch or so. The lap should then be turned partly around and another stroke made. This crosses the lines, providing a suitable surface for the embedding of the abrasive medium. Next, prepare the side of the lap. This is done by drawing the lap on the file in a direction parallel to the hole in the lap. Continue in this manner until the entire circumference is filed

Boxwood laps. Boxwood laps are used for putting a high polish on steel. We may use the slide rest in turning the boxwood in the same manner as we did in preparing the cast-iron and bell-metal laps. It is important that the grain of the wood run parallel with the hole in the lap so that the end of the grain touches the work. The lap is filed on the face only with a Number 0 file.

Preparing the grinding material. Now that the laps are ready, the preparation of the grinding medium is next in order. We proceed as follows:

Apply a small quantity of oilstone powder to the first compartment of the three-compartment polishing block. Add a little watch oil and mix with a small knife or spatula until a thin paste is produced. Place the pivot polisher on the lathe and adjust the lap spindle so that it stands at the same height from the bed as the lathe spindle. Adjust the index at the base of the polisher to ½ degree, so as to give the staff a slight taper toward the end when the grinding takes place. With the belting so fitted that the grinding surface of the lap and the surface of the staff rotate in opposite directions to each other, feed the lap up to the work by means of the hard-rubber knob at the rear. Apply thinly but evenly the oilstone paste to the lap and grind the balance seat. Continue the grinding until the balance just fits the seat. Be sure the undercutting is deep enough so that the corner of the lap does not touch the staff. If this is the case the balance can be riveted true and flat when the staff is finished. Next, grind the collet axis to size; after which, grind that portion of the staff between the cone of the pivot and the collet seat.

Grinding and polishing a cone pivot. Clean the work of the grinding material with a piece of pith previously dipped in benzole and hold it against the staff. Finish cleaning with a dry piece of pith. For the cone pivot, the polisher is set with the spindle at right angles to the pivot with the index set at 0 degree. It is further adjusted so that the center of the lap stands above the pivot as shown in Figure 18. This reduces the straight portion of the pivot perfectly cylindrical and forms the cone at the same time. The shape of the cone can be varied by raising or lowering the spindle of the polisher.

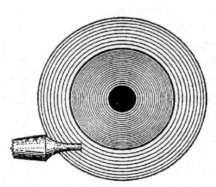

Figure 18. Method of polishing conical pivot.

Instead of the cast-iron lap we now use a bell-metal lap and a grinding medium of crocus   Reduce the pivot, frequently trying the jewel until it fits rather closely. Now remove the bell-metal lap and fit in its place a boxwood lap and polish the pivot, using a paste of diamantine and oil previously prepared on the top section of the polishing block. Continue the polishing until the pivot fits the jewel freely.

The slope between the collet axis and the cone of the pivot may now be smoothed further by holding a jasper slip in the hand. It is then polished with a boxwood slip and diamantine.

Turning hub and roughing out lower end of staff. Now that the upper end of the staff is finished we next turn with the hand graver a long slope from the balance seat to the lower end of the staff. With the pivot polisher set at the necessary angle, grind the slope for most of its length, using oilstone powder and oil. Smooth further with jasper slip and polish with boxwood lap, diamantine, and oil.

Next, cut out roughly the lower part with a graver slightly flattened at the point   Leave the hub a little longer than the finished staff is to be and the roller axis a little larger.

Cut off the staff and measure the overall length   The staff is, of course, a little too long. Place the collet axis in a split chuck and stone off the lower end until the staff is worked down to the correct length. Remove the staff and remeasure the overall length between the calipers of the Boley gauge as many times as is required, taking only a little off the end at a time so that the staff will not be made too short. This is positively the most exact method of bringing a staff to the correct length. Any other method, such as measuring back from a predetermined amount of extra length and cutting off after the work is cemented, is likely to result in errors

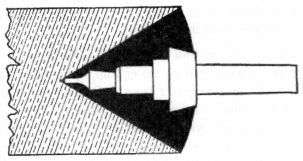

Figure 19.   Cement chuck.

The cement chuck. The staff having been brought to the correct length we are now ready for the cement chuck. A screw brass tightly screwed in a chuck must have a center turned in it, deep enough to take the staff up to and including the hub. Figure 19 shows the center with the staff in place and properly secured in the cement.

Setting the staff in the cement chuck. Place a small alcohol lamp under the cement brass. Heat sufficiently so that the brass will melt the cement and fill the center, at the same time running the lathe slowly. While the cement is still soft, insert the staff with the thumb and first finger. Again keeping the lathe in motion, reheat the brass until the cement adheres to the staff. Holding the staff in place with a hollowed-out piece of pegwood resting on the T rest, continue running the lathe until the cement is slightly cooled. Now, true up the staff while the cement is still soft by resting the pointed end of the pegwood on the T rest and bringing the pointed end against the roller axis. The T rest must be placed at an angle so that we may first hold the staff in place while allowing the cement to cool. The truing follows immediately by holding the pegwood in front of and at a right angle to the staff.

Turning the lower end of the staff. Turn the lower end of the staff, measuring from the end up to the roller seat, and bring the hub to the correct length. Reduce the roller axis to 0.1 of a millimeter of the correct diameter. Set the pivot polisher in position with the index adjusted to ½ degree taper and grind the roller axis until the roller table slides on and wedges tight at a distance about two thirds the way up to the hub. The pivot is next turned and polished as per instructions already given.

The staff is now removed from the cement chuck. Fill the boiling pan or test tube with alcohol and boil off cement.

Finishing the ends of the pivots. The ends of the pivots have not yet been finished but it is well first to try the staff in the watch and test for end shake, so we may know better in what manner to proceed. Since the measurement for the length was made without allowance for end shake, it usually follows that a slight touching up of the ends of the pivots is needed. To accomplish this, place the staff in a split chuck and flatten each end slightly, using a hard Arkansas slip. Polish further with a jasper slip and finally finish with a hardened steel burnisher and round the corners slightly.

COMMON ERRORS IN STAFF MAKING

Beginners are very apt to overlook certain important details in the turning of a staff. One of the most common is the absence of a square shoulder for the roller seat, so that the roller table will not lie flat to the full diameter of the hub. Undercutting for this purpose is not objectionable, for many watch factory staffs are made in this manner. In like manner the balance wheel should fit the staff, that is, flat to the full diameter of the hub

The collet axis, the balance axis, and the roller axis should show a definite taper so that the parts in question will fit properly This is easily attained with the pivot polisher, for the instrument may be set to the desired taper. In using the hand graver, the eye must be trained to recognize a suitable taper.

The straight portion of the pivots should be cylindrical and not tapering as we sometimes find them, and the cones should be shaped alike Again these conditions are made possible with the pivot polisher and likewise more difficult to attain without it. Satisfactory undercutting at the top of the balance seat is also important.

Success will be realized if the beginner will pay strict attention to detail, and it will be found that staff making is not as difficult as some workmen would have you believe

Problems

1. What gravers are needed in turning a staff ?

2. How do you measure for a staff ?

3. Explain in detail the hardening and tempering of the steel for staff making

4. Name the steps in turning the upper end of a staff in their proper order

5. How do you go about bringing the staff to the proper length ?

6. Must the staff run absolutely true in the cement chuck ?

7. Name the points of particular importance in staff making.

CHAPTER FOUR

Pivoting

SUCCESS in pivoting depends largely on the quality of the drills and in keeping the drills sharp. It is better to drill the pinions without tempering, yet there are times when tempering must be resorted to, and in such cases a small copper wire shaped as shown in Figure 20 may be used. The leaves of the pinion are held in a pin vise or parallel pliers to prevent the heat from spreading to that part while the copper is heated over an alcohol lamp. The end of the pinion is tempered to a blue color.

The pinion may be centered in the split chuck if it runs true; otherwise, the cement chuck must be used. Face off the pivot to the square shoulder and turn a small center. Place the pivot drill in a pin vise and drill a hole, which should be a little deeper than the length of the average pivot. Should the drill cease to cut, sharpen it immediately. A dull drill is apt to burnish the bottom of the hole, presenting a serious problem Should this happen, flatten the end of the drill, which usually results in the drill cutting again. The hole having been drilled to a satisfactory depth, secure a piece of pivot wire in a pin vise, and file sufficiently to just start and hang in the hole in the pinion Caution should be exercised in filing the wire to show as little taper as possible.

Roll the wire as the filing takes place so as to leave the wire round. Finish with the Arkansas slip. Next, force the wire in the hole, cut off the wire with the cutting pliers, and tap the plug with a small hammer, thereby forcing the plug securely in the hole. The pivot is turned nearly to size with the hand graver and finished to the proper size as already

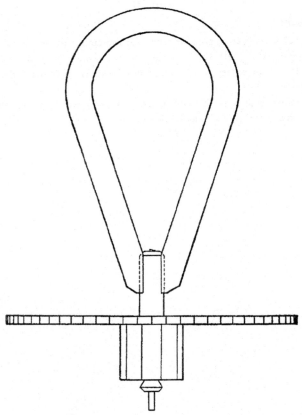

Figure 20. Copper wire in position for tempering pinion.

explained. It is advisable to undercut the square shoulder slightly before polishing in order to keep the corner sharp as shown in Figure 21.

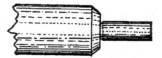

Figure 21.

Problems

1. What are the important points to remember in drilling a pinion for repivoting?

2. If a drill ceases to cut what may be done so that the drill will cut again?

3. What would be the most likely reason for a pivot working loose when turning with the graver?

CHAPTER FIVE

Fitting Balance Springs

IN FITTING balance springs the first procedure is to determine the number of vibrations of the balance per minute. This may be found in any watch fitted with a second hand by first dividing the number of teeth in the fourth wheel by the number of leaves in the escape pinion; then, by multiplying the quotient by twice the number of teeth in the escape wheel, we have ascertained the number of vibrations of the balance per minute.

For example, the fourth wheel has 80 teeth; the escape pinion has 8 leaves; the escape wheel has 15 teeth.

$$\frac{80 \times 30}{8} = 300 \text{ vibrations of the balance per minute}$$

Other examples are as follows:

$$\frac{72 \times 30}{8} = 270 \text{ vibrations per minute}$$

$$\frac{64 \times 30}{8} = 240 \text{ vibrations per minute}$$

In watches where the fourth wheel does not register seconds we have to go back to the center wheel, as shown in the following examples:

$$\frac{54 \times 50 \times 48 \times 30}{6 \times 6 \times 6} = 18,000 \text{ vibrations per hour}$$

$$\frac{64 \times 66 \times 60 \times 30}{8 \times 8 \times 6} = 19,800 \text{ vibrations per hour}$$

Fitting a Flat Spring

In fitting a flat spring to a watch, it is necessary to know the proper size. This is determined by centering the spring to the balance jewel as shown in Figure 22. The correct radius is located on the first coil that stands inside the inner regulator pin. Next, we desire to determine the approximate strength, which may be found by suspending the balance and spring an inch or two above the bench. If the distance between the point where the spring is held by the tweezers and the rim of the balance is ½ inch, the spring is approximately of the strength desired. It does not matter if the balance is large or small; the distance remains practically the same. Of course, this does not necessarily decide that a particular spring is to be used, but it does eliminate all unnecessary attempts at vibrating a spring that is positively unsuited for a balance.

After trying several springs, finally selecting one that conforms to the above test, the next procedure is to vibrate the spring. This can be done by counting the vibrations or by using an instrument commonly known as a *vibrator*. Since nearly all watches of recent years are made with a

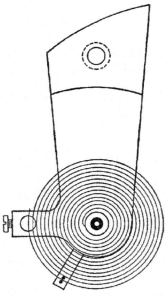

Figure 22. Method for determining correct size of flat balance spring.

300-beats-per-minute train, it is convenient to use the vibrator, about which more will be written in the next paragraph. For the other trains it will be necessary to count the vibrations, using a watch of known accuracy. The counting is done with every vibration that takes place in a clockwise direction; that is, the return vibration is not counted. The usual practice is to suspend the balance and spring by means of tweezers supported in the lathe bed. The lower pivot of the balance staff rests on the watch crystal. Thus, counting for one minute there would be 150 counts for a 300-beat train, 135 counts for a 270-beat train, etc

The vibrator. Vibrators may be purchased from material houses or may be made from an old balance and spring properly timed. Material catalogs may be consulted if the horologist desires to make his own instrument.

The method of using the vibrator is that of comparison—that is, watching the balance spring to be vibrated and the vibrator balance and noting whether or not both vibrate in unison We may slide the tweezers as much as a half a coil in toward the center of the spring or out a quarter of a coil toward the outside without altering the radius too much for a satisfactory fitting of the spring.

Having found a spring that vibrates properly, break it off one quarter of a coil beyond the vibrating point. Next the spring is pinned in at the stud and the balance bridge with balance and spring attached is placed in the watch for the final timing.

Fitting the Breguet Spring

The fitting of the Breguet spring to a watch involves all of the work of fitting a flat spring, plus the forming of the

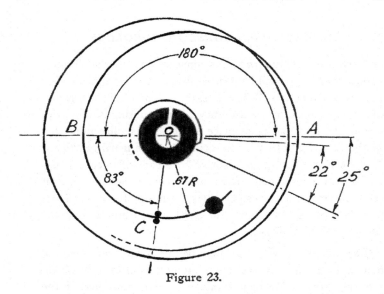

Figure 23.

overcoil. The diameter need not be so exacting; however, it should not be larger than one half of the diameter of the balance, including half of the screws.

We shall assume that the watch in need of a new spring is ideally suited to the Lossier terminal shown in Figure 23. The procedure is as follows: Vibrate the spring in the flat and break off the spring about two millimeters beyond the vibrating point. The length of the active portion of the overcoil must be determined and for this we must resort to a bit of calculation. We desire to find the length of the portion *BC* and *AB* (Figure 23). The following formula gives us the length of *BC*.

Number 1:

$$BC = \frac{2\,CO \times 3.14 \times 83}{360}$$

The radius CO multiplied by 2 gives us the diameter of that part of the overcoil concentric to O. Hence the diameter 2 CO multiplied by 3.14 gives us the circumference, which in turn is divided by 360 to determine the length of 1 degree. Multiplying the length of 1 degree by 83 degrees gives us the length of BC.

We now desire to know the length of AB, which, when added to BC, gives us the total length of the curve.

Number 2.

$$AB = \frac{(AO + OB)\ 3.14}{2}$$

Since $AO + OB$ equals the diameter and since one half of the circumference is required, it is only necessary to multiply $AO + OB$ by 3 14 to give the circumference and divide by 2.

Now, taking a practical example, let us suppose that the diameter of the spring is 8 millimeters. The radius would be 4 millimeters According to the elements of the curve, CO is .67 of the radius. Thus:

$$CO = 4 \times .67 = 2.68\ \text{mm}.$$

Substituting this value for CO in equation *Number 1* we may determine the angular distance for BC.

$$BC = \frac{5.36 \times 3.14 \times 83}{360} = 3\ 88\ \text{mm}.$$

Substituting again for equation *Number 2* we learn the length of AB.

$$AB = \frac{(2.68 + 4)\ 3\ 14}{2} = 10.48\ \text{mm}.$$

For the full length we add 3.88 and 10.48, giving us 14.36 millimeters.

We now grasp the spring at the point intended for the regulator pins and slide the spring along a scale in order to determine the actual length of the curve, allowing for sufficient extra length for the spring to reach the stud. It is permissible to make a slight mark at this point to indicate the starting point of the curve.

Raising the overcoil. We are now ready to raise the overcoil. This is accomplished with rather heavy tweezers. Grasp the spring with the tweezers about 25 degrees from that point where the inward bend starts. Hold the spring tightly and press into a piece of softwood until the outer coil takes on the shape shown in Figure 24. Turn the spring over and, measuring 22 degrees from the first bend, bend again until the outer coil lies level with the body of the spring, Figure 25. Bring in the raised portion so that the overcoil takes the form shown in Figure 23. To form the overcoil, tweezers of many shapes are desirable. These are shown in Figure 26. Alterations should be made gradually, being careful not to bend the spring too much, for in so doing, the

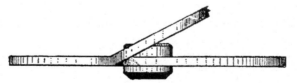

Figure 24. First bend in forming overcoil.

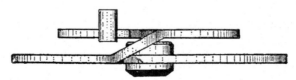

Figure 25. First and second bends in forming overcoil.

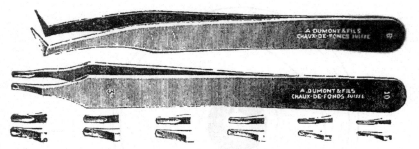

Figure 26.   Balance spring tweezers.

spring is liable to be considerably weakened and possibly broken.

The Lossier curve is not adaptable to most small watches for the reason that the curve is brought in nearer to the central portion of the total mass than these watches will permit. However, the above analysis may be used as a basis for calculating other forms, since the length of the curve does not vary very much. The forms more adaptable to present-day small watches are shown in Figures 27 and 28. In Figure 27 note that the radius of the overcoil along the path of the regulator pins is three fourths of the radius of the spring. The length of the curve is 180 degrees plus 20 degrees. Again in Figure 28 the portion of the overcoil at the regulator pins is placed in a position nearly in line with the full radius of the spring. In this type, the curve usually takes the form shown in the illustration and the bend for the overcoil starts at a point opposite the regulator pins.

Converting a Flat Spring into a Breguet

In order to obtain a closer position and isochronal rate in a watch originally fitted with a flat spring, it is sometimes desirable to make the spring over into a Breguet. In many

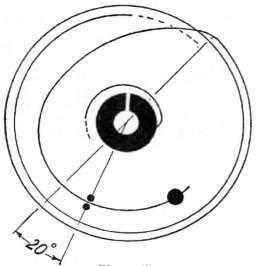

Figure 27.

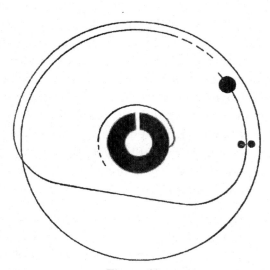

Figure 28.

watches where there is room enough under the balance bridge this can be done without much difficulty. The curve suitable for a case of this kind is composed of quadrants of two circles connected by a straight line as shown in Figure 29. The radii of the circles *A* and *B* are equal to about one half of the radius of the spring. Owing to the spiral nature of the spring the radius of the circle *B* is a little longer than that of circle *A*. The dotted line *CC* shows the outer coil of the flat spring and the solid line *DD* shows the same coil after it was formed into a Breguet. Figure 30 shows the same spring with the circles and dotted lines removed. A clearer picture of its relative form is thus realized. The only change to be made to the watch is to shorten the regulator pins and raise the stud. The curve is

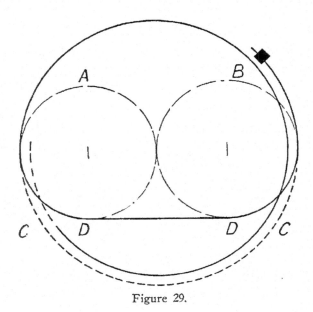

Figure 29.

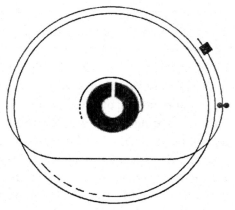

Figure 30.

theoretically correct and if properly executed it will be found to be equal to any type of overcoil.

Eccentric Motion of the Spring

After a spring has been fitted to a watch an eccentric vibration may be observed due to a faulty form of the overcoil. The rules for correcting the eccentric motion are as follows:

1. If the eccentric motion takes place opposite the regulator pins (as in a flat spring), bring in part of the overcoil toward the center of the spring.

2. If the eccentric motion takes place on the same side as the regulator pins, move part of the overcoil back into the main body of the spring.

Truing Balance Springs

The attainment of successful balance-spring truing comes only with continued practice and patience. It is one of those accomplishments that are difficult to teach through the printed page. For this reason we shall make only a few general statements as to the manipulative operations.

In truing the round it is never necessary to manipulate the spring beyond the first quarter of the inner coil, assuming that the spring is true except for that portion which is likely to be out as a result of pinning in at the collet. Figure 31 shows a spring divided into quarters. The sections are referred to as *first quarter, half, third quarter,* and *pinning point.* The spring may be wide at or near any of these points and the procedure in truing consists of pushing or twisting the spring in the desired directon. The dotted lines in Figure 32 show the manipulating required to bring the spring true in the round.

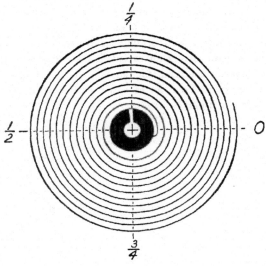

Figure 31.

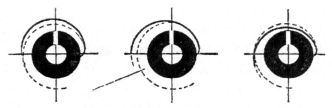

Figure 32. Dotted lines indicate manner in which the balance spring is twisted to true in the round.

In truing the flat the spring is pushed down or raised up at those points that are high or low.

Problems

1. Give the formula for determining the number of beats per minute of a watch.

2. How do you determine the correct size of a flat spring for a given watch?

3. How do you determine the correct size of a Breguet spring?

4. What is the correct length of a Lossier outer curve if the diameter of the balance spring is 6.5 millimeters?

5. How do you go about forming the overcoil?

6. How do you correct an eccentric motion of the spring that takes place opposite the regulator pins?

7. How do you correct an eccentric motion that takes place on the same side as the pins?

CHAPTER SIX

Escapement Adjusting

IN THIS study of the lever escapement we are particularly concerned with practical benchwork; that is, the placing in good order the escapement of a given watch It is important, however, that we have some understanding of the theoretical principles involved and we shall indulge, therefore, in as much theory and escapement design as is necessary to aid in the execution of practical repair problems

The importance of understanding the escapement cannot be overestimated. Large pocket watches often function quite satisfactorily with faulty escapements but with small wrist watches it is very different. The escapement in small ladies' watches must be practically perfect. Since the larger per cent of the watches that are brought in for repair today are wrist watches there is need for greater skill in escapement work. Inadequate knowledge results only in an endless amount of trouble with watches that stop persistently, though perhaps only occasionally. Erratic rates, too, can be traced to defective escapements.

Wheel and Pallet Action

The best way to obtain a practical understanding of the escapement is to proceed step by step, studying the separate functions, after which the escapement action as a whole will be analyzed Our attention will first be directed to the problem of banking the escapement to the drop.

Banking to the drop. The term "banked to the drop" means that the banking pins are turned in such a position that a tooth of the escape wheel will slide past the letting-off corner of a pallet, thereby permitting the lever to reach the opposite banking pin.

In order to effect a banked-to-the-drop condition, it is first necessary to turn in both banking pins. The impulse face of one pallet will now show contact with the impulse face of a tooth of the escape wheel, but owing to the fact that the banking pins have been turned in, the tooth is unable to pass the letting-off corner of the pallet Let us assume that the impulse faces of the receiving pallet and a tooth show contact. Turn the banking pin, against which the lever now rests, away from the line of centers slowly until a tooth passes the letting-off corner of the receiving pallet. At this instant another tooth will lock on the locking face of the discharging pallet. Next, move the lever to the opposite banking pin, resulting in a contact being shown between the impulse faces of the discharging pallet and a tooth. Turn the banking pin, against which the lever rests, away from the line of centers until the tooth drops as already explained, and the job of banking to the drop is completed

DROP LOCK

The extent of the lock on the pallets after an escapement has been banked to the drop is called drop lock. This lock takes place the instant a tooth drops on the locking face of a pallet

In Swiss watches and some American wrist watches it is not practical to bank the escapement to the drop because of the fact that the banking pins are not supplied with eccentric screws. In this case the usual practice is to slowly move the lever until the escape tooth drops and at the same instant cease moving the lever and take note of the extent of the lock on the pallets. A slight additional motion of the lever should be required before the lever will reach its bank, which is, of course, beyond that of drop lock. The additional motion is called *slide* and will be considered further in the later portion of this chapter.

Correct drop lock. Drop lock is a varying quantity, depending on the position of the pallet stones in the pallet arm, but it should be as light as possible consistent with proper safety in action. A drop lock of 1½ or 2 degrees is the amount usually adopted for pocket watches, whereas 2 or 3 degrees is allowed for wrist watches

Altering the drop locks. If the drop locks are too light or unsafe, a deeper lock can be had by moving out one or both pallets. Likewise if the drop locks are too deep a lighter lock can be had by moving in one or both pallets It will be observed that when one pallet is moved the lock is changed on both pallets and any alteration of the pallets should always be followed by rebanking to the drop

Out of angle. The lever should move an equal distance on either side of the line of centers. If the lever does not move an equal distance the lever is said to be "out of angle." If the drop locks are deep, out of angle can be corrected by moving *in* the pallet on the side where the lever's angular motion is shorter from the line of centers. If the drop locks are light, out of angle can be corrected by moving *out* the pallet on the side where the lever's angular motion is longer from the line of centers. If the drop locks are satisfactory, out of angle (if slight) can be corrected by carefully bending the lever as close as possible to the pallet staff. This can be done by holding the lever with a small pair of pliers and bending it with the thumb and first finger. And remember— rebank the escapement to the drop after each alteration.

THE DRAW

The force that keeps the lever against its bank is called "draw." It exists because of the inclination or slant of the pallet's locking face and the shape of the tooth. It will be observed in Figure 36 that the receiving pallet inclines in the direction toward the pallet center and the discharging pallet inclines in the same direction but away from the pallet center, thus forming the angle for draw. A draw of 12 degrees is considered sufficient by most horologists.

Examining the draw. Take a watch oiler or similar small tool and lift the lever away from its bank, but not far enough to cause the escapement to unlock. Now release the lever, and in so doing the lever will, if the escapement is correct, return immediately to its bank Try this again with the lever against the opposite banking. The lever should at once return to its bank.

The purpose of draw is to avoid unnecessary friction between the guard pin and the roller table. When the watch receives a jolt the lever is thrown away from its bank and the guard pin comes in contact with the roller table, but the action of draw causes the lever to return at once to its bank. Draw should be sufficient to effect the return of the lever to its bank for all ordinary conditions. If the draw is excessive, there will be an unnecessary recoil of the escape wheel, causing a condition whereby too much of the force of the balance and spring is used in unlocking the escapement. The result is a waste of power and a shorter arc of motion of the balance.

Altering the draw. As a rule want of draw is due to insufficient angle of a pallet stone. In most cases the jewel may be tilted in the pallet arm. If the jewel fits tightly, a thinner jewel may be substituted or the slot may be widened to give the jewel more angle.

THE DROP

Drop is defined as the free motion of the escape wheel at the time when one tooth passes the letting-off corner of a pallet and another tooth comes in contact with the locking face of the opposite pallet. Drop may be also defined as the distance a tooth of the escape wheel travels without doing any work.

Examining the drop. With a tooth locked on the receiving pallet observe the space that separates the letting-off corner of the discharging pallet from the heel of the tooth. Now move the lever to the opposite banking pin, thereby causing a tooth to lock on the discharging pallet. Next observe the space that separates the letting-off corner of the receiving pallet from the heel of the tooth.

Of course, the drop should be equal, but we do not always find it so. A small drop on the receiving pallet is called "close outside," and a small drop on the discharging pallet is called "close inside." These errors call for correction. If close inside, tip one or both pallets away from the pallet staff. If close outside, tip one or both pallets toward the pallet staff.

Usually, moving one pallet is all that is necessary. The question may arise as to which pallet to move. This would depend largely on the condition of the draw, the drop locks, and the angular motion of the lever from the line of centers, for we shall soon learn that whenever a pallet is shifted for any reason all of the above conditions are altered.

SHAKE

Shake is defined as that space separating the letting-off corner of the pallet from the heel of a tooth when the opposite pallet is locked at the lowest locking corner. Shake is similar to drop except that the examination for shake occurs at the time when the tooth is locked at the lowest locking corner of the pallet When moving the lever away from its bank but not enough to unlock the escapement, it will be observed that a slight recoil of the escape wheel has taken place. This action lessens the space between the letting-off corner of the pallet and the heel of the tooth, showing that shake is always less than drop. If an escapement has no shake the watch will stop

THE LIFT

Modern escapements have a total lift of 8½ degrees. The amount of lift separately on tooth and pallet is designed in varying proportions in different makes of watches. The lift in a club-tooth escapement is a very complicated action and requires considerable study to understand it. It will be noticed that the lift does not function exactly the same on both pallets. On the receiving pallet the wheel moves up as also does the pallet and the pallet's locking corner moves with greater velocity than the letting-off corner. On the discharging pallet the condition is reversed and the wheel moves

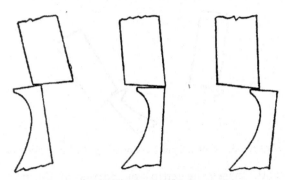

Figure 33. Lift on receiving pallet.

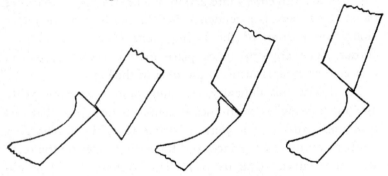

Figure 34. Lift on discharging pallet.

down while the pallet moves up. Also, the letting-off corner of the discharging pallet moves with greater velocity than the locking corner.

A good action between the wheel and pallets is shown in Figures 33 and 34. Note that as the tooth leaves the locking faces of the pallets, the toe of the tooth shows contact only with the pallet's impulse faces. Contact in this manner continues completely across the pallets until finally the two impulse faces meet nearly parallel, and after that the heel

Figure 35.   Curved pallet stones by A. Lange & Son.

of the tooth passes the letting-off corner of the pallets. The heel of the tooth comes into action quicker on the discharging pallet; also there is a tendency for the tooth to move faster along that portion of the lifting plane near the letting-off corner. The opposite takes place on the receiving pallet; that is, the action is faster at the start of the lift.

To obviate this difficulty, A. Lange and Sons some years ago made watches with escapements so designed that the receiving pallet had a convex lifting face, the discharging pallet a concave lifting face, and the lifting faces on the teeth were also curved (Figure 35). This system, it will be observed, would cause the lifting action of the tooth to function at a more nearly constant velocity.

Loss in the lift.   There is a definite amount of loss of lift on the discharging pallet of the club-tooth escapement. This is shown in Figure 36. *BC* is a straight line but the escape wheel describes the circle *DD*; hence these lines must deviate from each other. In order that $5\frac{1}{2}$ degrees of lifting take place, a lifting angle of $6\frac{1}{4}$ degrees is required of the discharging pallet. However, this loss of lift is a problem to be reckoned with principally in the equidistant pallets. In the circular pallets the loss of lift is very little for the reason

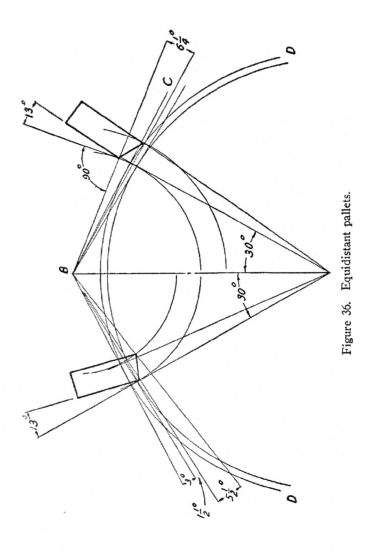

Figure 36. Equidistant pallets.

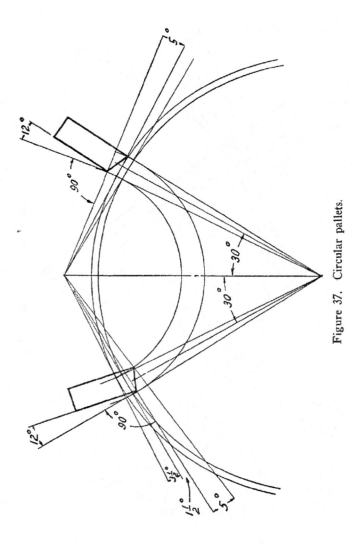

Figure 37. Circular pallets.

that the tangents are planted mid-way between the locking and letting-off corners of the pallets (Figure 37). The loss of lift in the semitangental escapement is also small, usually amounting to about one-half degree (Figure 40).

The Fork and Roller Action

In this study of the lever escapement we have up till now concerned ourselves with such factors as banking to the drop; drop lock, draw, drop, shake, and the lifting action These, it is observed, constitute the escape wheel and pallet action. We are now ready to investigate the fork and roller action which is quite a study in itself. There is, however, a definite relationship between the two actions and the last mentioned cannot be successfully studied without taking particular account of the former Hence the wheel and pallet action in its entirety was outlined first and it is assumed that our escapement is in satisfactory adjustment up to this point.

The lever's angular motion. We have stated that the combined lift on the tooth and pallets is $8\frac{1}{2}$ degrees. Adding this to a drop lock of $1\frac{1}{2}$ degrees, the total angular motion of the lever becomes 10 degrees. The lever's angular motion of 10 degrees should be all that is necessary for the roller jewel to pass in and out of the fork satisfactorily without catching. Now, placing the balance in the watch, we are ready to try the tests for the safety locks. These are the *guard* safety test and the *corner* safety test Using a strong eyeglass in making the tests, we proceed as follows.

SAFETY LOCK TESTS

Guard safety test. Rotate the balance so that the roller jewel stands outside of the fork and with the first finger

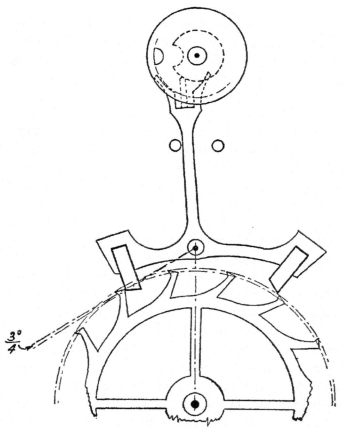

Figure 38. Guard safety test.

hold the balance in this position. Now, with a watch oiler or similar small tool, lift the lever away from its bank, thereby causing the guard finger to come in contact with the edge of the safety roller as shown in Figure 38. With the lever held in this position examine the remaining lock on the pallet. This remaining lock is called a safety lock and it should

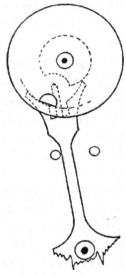

Figure 39.
Corner safety test.

represent one half of drop lock or ¾ degree of lock. The test should next be tried on the opposite pallet and a similar lock should be found.

Corner safety test. Starting with the roller jewel in the fork slot, rotate the balance slowly until such time that one tooth passes the letting-off corner of a pallet and another tooth comes in contact with the locking face of the opposite pallet. A slight additional motion applied to the balance will bring the roller jewel in a position opposite to the slot corner. With the balance held in this position, lift the lever away from its bank, thereby causing the slot corner to come in contact with the roller jewel as shown in Figure 39. With the lever held thus, examine the remaining or safety lock. Try this test on the opposite pallet and if the safety lock is the same on both pallets the lever's angular motion from the line of centers is practically equal.

The safety lock shown by the corner test should be the same as the safety lock shown by the guard test; that is, the safety locks from both sources should show ¾ degree of lock. NOTE—Although this is correct in theory it does not always work out in practice. If the safety lock shown by the corner test is less than the safety lock shown by the guard test—that is, if the corner freedom is greater than the guard freedom—no harm results, provided that the locking of both pallets is safe on all of the teeth of the escape wheel. *How-*

ever, if the corner freedom is less than the guard freedom, the roller jewel is apt to catch on the tips of the horns of the fork, causing the watch to stop.

The curve test. To test an escapement for the error stated above, we use what is called the curve test. To apply this test it is necessary to rotate the balance so that the roller jewel stands completely past the horns of the fork. Next, lift the lever away from its bank, thereby causing the guard finger to come in contact with the safety roller and, while the lever is held thus, turn the balance so that the roller jewel will move toward the fork slot. If the roller jewel passes the horns of the fork and enters the slot, the escapement is satisfactory as far as this test is concerned. If the roller jewel catches on the tips of the horns, a number of faulty conditions could be present. The most common are: guard finger too short, roller jewel advanced too far, or lever too long

The drop locks being correct, it is now apparent that the guard, corner, and curve tests aid in determining the correct length of the lever. It is common practice in escapement work to lengthen the lever by stretching it or to shorten it by grinding the horns as the case may require. So bear in mind that the condition of the drop locks is first taken account of and the fork and roller action afterward.

Slide

Up to this point in our discussion, the escapement has been banked to the drop. The subject of slide is next in order. The opening of the banking pins beyond that of drop lock is called slide. Slide should be large enough to permit freedom for escaping; usually ½ degree is considered sufficient. Any amount more than this only increases the angular motion of the lever and its connection with the balance, resulting in an increased unlocking resistance, a shorter arc of motion of the balance, and poor timekeeping. The banking pins should be placed as far as possible away from the pallet center so as to lessen the strain on the lever pivots should the escapement overbank.

Slide is the last adjustment, the finishing touches, so to speak, in escapement adjusting.

The Theoretically Correct Escapement

As sort of summary of our discussion of the escapement, let us consider the specifications of a correctly designed escapement.

When banked to the drop, the specifications should read as follows:

Drop lock	$1\frac{1}{2}°$	
Safety lock	$\frac{3}{4}°$	
Corner freedom	$\frac{3}{4}°$	$(1\frac{1}{2}° — \frac{3}{4}° = \frac{3}{4}°)$
Guard freedom	$\frac{3}{4}°$	$(1\frac{1}{2}° — \frac{3}{4}° = \frac{3}{4}°)$

With slide added, the specifications now read:

Total lock	$2\ °$	$(1\frac{1}{2}° + \frac{1}{2}° = 2°)$
Safety lock	$\frac{3}{4}°$	
Corner freedom	$1\frac{1}{4}°$	$(2° — \frac{3}{4}° = 1\frac{1}{4}°)$
Guard freedom	$1\frac{1}{4}°$	$(2° — \frac{3}{4}° = 1\frac{1}{4}°)$
Slide lock	$\frac{1}{2}°$	$(2° — 1\frac{1}{2}° = \frac{1}{2}°)$
Drop lock	$1\frac{1}{2}°$	$(2° — \frac{1}{2}° = 1\frac{1}{2}°)$

Drawing the Lever Escapement

This chapter would not be complete without adding a few lines about drawing the lever escapement. We have selected

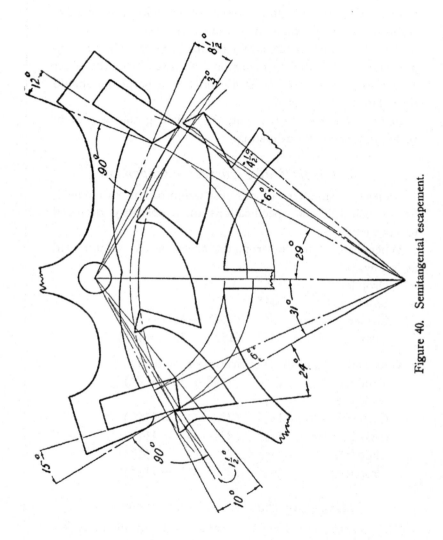

Figure 40. Semitangental escapement.

for this purpose the semitangental escapement shown in Figure 40, as it comprises the best and latest design in escapement construction.

The materials needed for drawing are: a drawing board, drawing instruments, pencil, large and small protractors, drawing paper, and India ink. A T square, two triangles, and a French curve would be desirable although not absolutely necessary.

Study the drawing thoroughly before starting. Note at what points the various angles originate. It is important, also, to make the drawing on a large scale so as to minimize the errors arising from imperfections in our drawing instruments. Students who have no knowledge of mechanical drawing would do well to read several chapters in any good textbook on mechanical drawing.

RECOMMENDED TEXTS:

Roberts, William E., *Beginning Mechanical Drawing.* The Manual Arts Press, Peoria, Illinois, 1943

Bennett, Charles A., *Beginning Problems in Mechanical Drawing.* The Manual Arts Press, Peoria, Illinois, 1934.

Practical Application of Escapement Tests

Knowledge of the several escapement tests will be of little value unless they reveal the necessary corrections to be made in defective escapements. The purpose of this section is, therefore, to show the application of the several tests as a guide to escapement alterations. All of the examples listed in the following pages are based on actual problems experienced and corrected by the writer in the course of practical work at the bench.

In all cases it is first assumed that the escapement was banked to the drop.

Adjustment 1.

> *Drop locks — correct*
> *Guard freedom — excessive*
> *Corner freedom — correct*

In this escapement the guard freedom was greater than the corner freedom. When the curve test was tried the roller jewel would catch on the horns of the fork. The correction consisted of flattening the end of the guard finger. For this purpose a punch should be ground so that the end will fit in the fork slot A very light tap with a small hammer will do the work. In some cases the guard pin may be lengthened by forcing it further through the piece in which the pin is placed. In this case, however, the pin could not be lengthened, and, besides, the crescent in the safety roller was rather wide. After flattening the guard finger the sides were stoned to provide the necessary guard freedom. The guard safety test, the corner safety test, and the curve test were tried and all tests were found satisfactory. The banking pins were opened for slide.

Adjustment 2.

> *Drop lock — correct*
> *Guard freedom — excessive*
> *Corner freedom — excessive*

When the guard test and the corner test were tried the pallets would recede from the tooth to such an extent that the impulse faces of both tooth and pallets would show contact; that is, the safety locks did not function on some of the teeth. Since the drop locks were correct the excessive guard and corner freedom suggested that the error was that of a short fork. The lever was therefore stretched and the guard test and corner test were again tried. It will be well to state at this time that the stretching should be done a very little at a time, frequently making use of the tests. To stretch a lever, place a small, flat-faced stump in the staking tool and lay the lever thereon. Using a punch with sides flattened, lightly tap the lever. If the lever becomes bent during the act of stretching, turn it over on the stump and give it another very light tap, using the same punch Having found the guard and corner tests satisfactory after stretching the lever, the banking pins are opened for slide.

Adjustment 3.

Drop locks — deep
Guard freedom — satisfactory
Corner freedom — satisfactory

Since the drop locks were deep, the first act was to move in both pallet stones and rebank to the drop. It was found after rebanking to the drop that the roller jewel would not pass in and out of the fork. The roller jewel was reset in a position a little nearer to the balance staff. Replacing the balance, the corner test was tried and the corner freedom was found to be correct, but when trying the guard test no guard freedom was found. This example being an escapement of the single roller type, the guard pin was bent away from the roller table. The guard test, the corner test, and the curve test were tried and all were found satisfactory, after which the banking pins were opened for slide.

Adjustment 4.

Drop locks — light
Guard freedom — none
Corner freedom — faulty

Since the drop locks were light the first act was to increase the drop lock. This made it necessary to spread the banking pins to a new banked-to-the-drop position. A proper guard freedom and safety lock were found when trying the guard test but when the corner test was tried the freedom was found to be excessive and the locking was not safe on all of the teeth. Examination showed that the roller jewel tipped slightly toward the staff. The roller jewel was reset in a position parallel with the staff and the corner test was again tried, this time showing the correct corner freedom and safety lock. As a final check-up, the guard, corner, and curve tests were tried and all were found satisfactory, after which slide was added.

Adjustment 5.

Drop locks — deep
Out of angle

When banked to the drop the escapement showed too much guard freedom on the side of the receiving pallet and practically correct freedom on the side of the discharging pallet. To correct the deep lock and to equalize the angular motion of the lever from the line of centers, the discharging pallet was moved in. The escapement was again banked to the drop and the guard and corner tests were tried, showing too much guard and corner freedom, also a complete absence of safety lock. The drop locks were considered passable, so the error was assumed to be that of a short fork. The lever was stretched and the guard and corner tests were tried, showing satisfactory guard and corner freedom and safety lock. The banking pins were opened for slide.

Adjustment 6.

Drop locks — satisfactory
Out of angle
Drop and shake — close outside

The drop locks being practically correct, the first act was to correct the condition of out of angle. As the out of angle was slight with the access of freedom on the side of the discharging pallet, the lever was bent in the direction toward the receiving pallet After banking to the drop and repeating the several tests, the lever was found equal with regard to the corner freedom, but the drop was still inequal, the condition being that of close outside. It will be noted that by bending the lever, the draw was increased, and for this reason it was decided that the receiving pallet should be tipped toward the pallet staff to equalize the drop. This was accordingly done and a test for draw followed, showing a satisfactory condition.   All tests were tried and found satisfactory. The banking pins were opened for slide.

Adjustment 7.

Drop locks — correct
Guard freedom — none
Corner freedom — none

After banking to the drop, this escapement did not show any guard and corner freedom Since the drop locks were correct it was reasoned that the lever was too long. The correction consists of grinding back the horns of the fork.

This is done by fitting to the lathe an iron wire, part of which is turned to fit the curve of the horns of the fork. Using oilstone powder and oil, the horns are ground by holding the lever with a pair of cutting pliers against the iron wire. Frequent applications of the corner test while grinding prevented any possibility of overdoing the correction. After grinding and polishing, the several tests showed a very satisfactory escapement action. The banking pins were opened for slide.

Adjustment 8.

Condition of escapement — satisfactory
Error — guard pin jams against roller table

In this example we have single roller type of escapement. After banking to the drop, the corner test was tried and found satisfactory. When the guard test was tried, the guard pin would jam or stick on the edge of the roller table. This error, responsible for frequent stopping, occurs occasionally in single roller escapements, but in double roller escapements only when the guard finger is loose or bent. The correction in the above example consisted of turning down and repolishing the edge of the roller table and advancing the guard pin. All tests showing satisfactory conditions, slide was added and the watch proved to be an excellent timekeeper.

Adjustment 9.

Drop locks — deep
Out of angle
Draw — wanting on both pallets

This escapement was out of angle, with the excessive guard freedom on the side of the receiving pallet, and since the drop locks were deep and the draw was deficient it was reasoned that all faulty conditions could be corrected by moving in the discharging pallet   The discharging pallet was accordingly moved in and after rebanking to the drop a thorough examination showed that the drop locks were correct; the lever's angular motion from the line of centers was equal and the draw was satisfactory.   This example should be remembered.   Errors of this kind occur quite frequently and the correction is easy and the results are certain.

Problems

1. What is meant by "banked to the drop"?
2. Define drop lock.
3. State in degrees the correct amount of drop lock.
4. What is meant by "out of angle"?
5. How do you correct out of angle?
6. Define draw
7. How do you examine draw?
8. Define drop.
9. How do you examine drop?
10. Define shake
11. What is the lift?
12. What are the characteristics of a good action of lift?
13. What is meant by the expression "loss in the lift"?
14. On what type of escapement is the loss in the lift greatest?
15. State in degrees the total angular motion of the lever when the escapement is banked to the drop.
16. Should a watch run when banked to the drop?
17. In what manner do you go about making the guard safety test? corner safety test? curve test?
18. What is the purpose of the guard safety test? corner safety test? curve test?

19. What do the above tests aid in determining, if the drop locks are correct?

20. Define slide

21. When is slide added?

22. Give the specifications for a correctly designed escapement, first without slide, secondly with slide.

23. Does altering the banking pins change the drop lock?

24. Define total lock.

25. Does altering the banking pins change the total lock?

26. How do you correct an escapement in which the drop locks are correct but there is an excessive guard and corner freedom?

27. What is the error in an escapement that has a deep lock yet the guard and corner freedom are satisfactory?

28 If the drop locks are light and the guard and corner tests show no freedom, what is the correct procedure to put the escapement in order?

29 The drop locks are deep and the escapement is out of angle with no guard and corner freedom on the side of the discharging pallet. There is, however, too much guard and corner freedom on the side of the receiving pallet. How would you go about correcting this escapement?

CHAPTER SEVEN

Cleaning and Oiling

Two methods are used in cleaning watches. The first that we shall consider is the older method generally referred to as the hand method. The second involves the use of the cleaning machine.

The Hand Method

In using the hand method we proceed as follows: After taking the movement apart string the larger pieces on a wire loop, place the pieces in benzine, benzole, or any other good cleaning preparation for several minutes. Remove and wash pieces in hot water, using castile soap and a soft brush. Rinse in clean water, dip in cyanide of potassium, rinse again in clean water, immerse in alcohol, and dry in warm sawdust. The same treatment is given to the wheels and other small pieces that can be strung on the wire loop, but separately, after the plates have been cleaned. The other small pieces such as the pallet fork and the jewels, may be held against a piece of hard pith or cork with a pair of tweezers especially prepared for the purpose and brushed thoroughly with a fine toothbrush previously dipped in benzole. After being brushed, the pieces are dipped in alcohol and allowed to dry on a sheet of watch paper. The balance must be cleaned separately. The usual method is to dip the balance first in

124

benzole, then in water followed by cyanide, again in water and finally in alcohol, after which it is dried in sawdust. The parts are now dry and the jewels should be rubbed with two pieces of pegwood, one which has been pointed so as to go through the holes and another that has been shaped to fit the cups of the jewels.

The watch having been cleaned, the assembling and oiling are next in order. Certain parts are oiled as the watch is put together. For example, the main spring is oiled in the barrel with clock oil. The winding mechanism, the escape wheel, the pallet jewels, and the hole jewels where cap jewels are used in connection are also oiled in the process of assembling. The train is oiled after the watch is assembled, also the center post that carries the cannon pinion. The roller jewel is *not* oiled.

The Watch-cleaning Machine

The newer method of cleaning watches with the cleaning machine has some advantages. It eliminates the use of cyanide. Instead, an especially prepared cleaning solution is used, together with water and a drying solution. The machine is particularly satisfactory for the cleaning of small pieces like the pallet fork, the jewels, and screws and has the further advantage of eliminating the use of sawdust.

Briefly, the procedure is as follows: Place the parts in the basket. There are provided several small spaces for the small pieces and one large space for the plates Lower the basket into the jar containing the cleaning solution and allow the motor to run for several minutes at a moderate speed. Throw off the cleaning solution by raising the basket sufficiently to clear the solution Lower the basket in a jar containing water and rinse off the cleaning solution. Next, lower the basket in the drying solution and run the motor as before. Finally, allow the basket to spin in a receptacle containing a lighted electric light bulb for a quick drying of the watch parts. Thus the cleaning job is completed.

Problems

1 Is it important that the jewels should be cleaned with pegwood?

2 What parts of a watch do you oil?

3. What parts should not be oiled?

4 Name some advantages in using the cleaning machine.

PART III

ADJUSTING

CHAPTER ONE

Preliminary Notes on Adjusting

THERE IS a greater demand for watches of accurate time-keeping qualities today than there was years ago. The railroads require that their employees' watches run within certain close limits and the complexity of modern life has shown a need for greater accuracy also. To repair watches so that close timing can be assured, a working knowledge of adjusting is necessary.

The horologist who has never been concerned about the theory and practice of adjusting has missed the real fascination and satisfaction of watch work. Aside from gaining pleasure for himself, the repairman who applies the principles of adjusting to his work will win the respect of his employer and the sincere appreciation of his customers

Adjusting consists in the execution of such manipulative operations of the balance spring and other parts as to cause a watch to function uniformly, the rate being within well-defined limits under various conditions. Adjusting is naturally divided into three branches: (1) position adjusting, (2) isochronal adjusting, and (3) temperature adjusting. These require independent methods of correction but in the final analysis all three are inseparable when the work of adjusting is completed.

General Observations

Before considering the more complex problems it will be well to outline briefly those conditions which must be as nearly perfect as possible before work can be attempted.

THE MAIN TRAIN

Close position and isochronal rating cannot be expected unless the main train is in first-class condition. Extreme variation is often caused by defects in any of the train wheels and especially in the center wheel and mainspring barrel. A correct amount of end shake and side shake is important. It is well, therefore, to examine a number of high-grade movements with regard to train freedom and note, also, the recoil of the escape wheel after the train runs down when winding the mainspring even to the slightest degree.

All train-wheel and balance pivots should be round and well polished. A pivot that is not perfectly round will function fairly well in a jewel hole that is round, but jewels frequently do not have perfectly round holes. To show the effect plainly, insert a three-cornered piece of steel in a jewel that has a perfectly round hole. The triangular piece, if it fits the jewel properly, will turn in the hole as perfectly as a well-rounded pivot, but if we change the jewel for one that is not round and repeat the experiment, the result will be different. The triangular piece will become wedged and will not turn. The effect exists in a lesser degree when an imperfect jewel and an out-of-round pivot are used together, yet the combined action of the two affects the time-keeping qualities of a watch

Furthermore, it is impossible to poise the balance if the pivots of the staff are not round, and in this connection we recommend the pivot polisher on all occasions where a balance pivot needs reducing or polishing. This lathe attachment forms the pivots perfectly round and cylindrical (assuming the machine is properly adjusted), and it does the work quickly and with a factorylike polish.

INFLUENCE OF THE LEVER ESCAPEMENT ON THE ADJUSTMENTS

The impulse communicated to the balance through the escapement should take place at the moment when the balance spring is at its state of rest, that is, at that moment when the spring is under no tension whatsoever. This ideal condition would permit the balance and spring to perform its arcs of vibration in the same time that a free balance and spring would perform these arcs. However, the mechanical means at one's disposal to keep the balance vibrating does not meet the above requirements and one is obliged to take account of the following laws.

1. An impulse delivered to a balance or pendulum before the point of rest will accelerate the vibrations.

2. An impulse delivered to a balance or pendulum after its point of rest will retard the vibrations.

This principle can be easily demonstrated with a simple pendulum. Impulse given to a pendulum before it reaches its point of rest causes it to arrive at the point of rest more quickly than if it were acted upon by gravity alone. Given impulse after reaching the point of rest results in driving the pendulum farther, resisting the force of gravity and at no particularly accelerated rate, if any Hence a retardation takes place and the greater the distance the impulse takes place after the point of rest, the greater is the retardation.

Now consider this factor in relation to the lever escapement. The total angular motion of the lever is 10 5 degrees, allowing for 2 degrees of lock. The relationship between the acting length of the lever and the roller jewel radius is 3.5 to 1. The total lifting angle or contact with the balance would be 3.5 × 10.5 or 36.75 degrees. Placing one half of this figure on either side of the line of centers we would have 18.375 degrees. However, the locking must be removed from that portion of contact before the line of centers (point of rest). Thus the impulse communicated before the line of centers would be 18.375 —(3.5 × 2) = 11.375 degrees. The impulse after the line of centers would be the full amount or 18.375 degrees.

According to the above analysis a retardation would result for the short arcs. Further retardation occurs because of the unlocking action, which is a serious resistance to the free motion of the balance. Hence it is clearly seen that a carefully adjusted escapement is of the utmost importance in the fine position and isochronal rating of a watch.

WEIGHT OF THE ESCAPE WHEEL AND PALLET FORK

The escape wheel should be as light as possible consistent with proper firmness. The sluggishness of a heavy escape wheel directly increases the inequality of the impulse between the receiving and discharging pallets owing to the inequality of the draw and the lift on the pallets

The lever, too, should be made as light as possible. It was formerly the practice of manufacturers to add a counterpoise to the lever, supposing that it was necessary to secure close position rating Research into the problem has demonstrated that this is not necessary; in fact, it can be shown that lightness of the lever is of much more importance. The counterpoise only gives the force at the circumference of the escape wheel more work to do and thus tends to make the actions of the escapement and balance more sluggish

MAINSPRINGS AND BALANCE MOTION

A mainspring unwinding in a barrel generally does not take place in a concentric manner. Were it possible that this ideal condition could be attained, there would be little or no friction between the coils and a more smooth and even motive power would result. This eccentricity in the act of unwinding varies with the type of brace or hook used on the outer end of the spring. Experience has shown that any type of hook that maintains a quarter turn of the external coil flat against the wall of the barrel gives good results and it is gratifying to note that more and more manufacturers are adopting some form of hook with this end in view.

It is important that the horologist use the very best mainsprings that money can buy. The superior performance of a good spring is so apparent in the position rating of a watch that no argument is necessary to convince the most skeptical. Springs that are set, even to a comparatively slight degree, should be replaced with new ones and the mainspring winder should always be used.

The proper arc of motion of the balance is 540 degrees when the watch is fully wound and lying in a horizontal position. Horologists experience a feeling of real satisfaction when a full balance arc is attained with the fitting of the weakest possible mainspring. It is an indication that the most even motive power will be maintained for the full 24 hours of running and that there will be only a slight falling-off of the balance arc at the end of a 24 hours run.

How to ascertain the arc of motion. The question may arise as to how we are able to ascertain this arc of motion. This the eye can be trained to recognize easily and at a glance by using the following method: Suppose the balance is at rest with the roller jewel in the fork slot midway between the banking pins. Now move the balance one half of a circle or 180 degrees and stop. Release the balance and the force of the spring will cause it to return to its point of rest and 180 degrees farther on the opposite side. The arc of motion would be 360 degrees. Again move the balance, three fourths of a circle or 270 degrees, and allow it to return on its own power to its point of rest and as far on the opposite side. The arc of motion is now 540 degrees and the balance will continue to vibrate between these points as long as the proper motive power is maintained.

The arms of the balance become visible at the moment the balance completes the arc of motion and starts in the opposite direction on its return vibration. It is, therefore, at that time when the balance stops that the arc of motion can be determined.

With the assistance of Figure 1, the problem can be more clearly explained in this manner: When the balance vibrates 180 degrees and returns to 0 degrees and continues as far on the opposite side—that is, when the arms are visible at 180 degrees and 0 degrees—the arc of motion is 360 degrees. When the

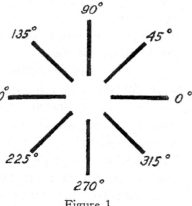

Figure 1.

balance vibrates 225 degrees and returns to 0 degrees and continues as far on the opposite side—that is, when the arms are visible first at 225 degrees and 45 degrees and on its return vibration at 135 degrees and 315 degrees (forming a cross at right angles)—the arc of motion is 450 degrees. When the balance vibrates 270 degrees and returns to 0 degrees and continues as far on the opposite side—that is, when the arms are visible at 270 degrees and 90 degrees— the arc of motion is 540 degrees.

The horologist should examine the balance arc in all positions and if the motion is faulty in certain positions the necessary corrections should be made before any adjustment to position or isochronism is attempted. Note carefully if there is any difference between the arcs of dial up and dial down. These positions should be equal. Note also the arcs of pendant up, pendant right, pendant left, and pendant down The arcs for the vertical positions should be the same although somewhat shorter than those for the two horizontal positions, owing to the increased friction on the balance pivots.

The arc of motion should never be longer than 540 degrees. Experience has shown that an arc longer than the above figure produces a very fast rate for the first few hours of running, after which time (the arcs becoming shorter) the watch functions at its normal rate.

THE POISE OF THE BALANCE

One of the most common causes of variation between positions is want of poise of the balance. The horizontal positions are not affected but the error in the vertical positions is considerable. The extent of the variation in the rate is in proportion to the extent of the error in poise.

If the excess of weight is on the lower side of the balance when at rest, the watch will lose when the arc of motion is greater than 450 degrees, and will gain when the arc is less.

If the weight is on the top side when the balance is at rest, the result will be reversed and the watch will gain when the arc of motion is greater than 450 degrees and will lose when the arc is less.

Nature of error due to want of poise. Let us assume that the excess of weight is on the lower side of the balance when at rest. Suppose the balance vibrates at an arc of almost 360 degrees, and in doing so the weight will stop near the top of the balance. The force of the spring in returning the balance to its point of rest will receive an added energy in that of gravity acting on the weight. This means that the spring will return to its point of rest a little more quickly than when acted upon by the force of the spring alone. Now assume that the weight, after having reached the bottom, continues the arc on the opposite side. The force of gravity acting on the weight is an added resistance to that of the spring; in other words, the result of an added weight is, in effect, the same as if a stronger spring were used and the arc will be performed more quickly.

Now suppose that the motion is increased to 540 degrees and in vibrating to this extent the weight starts from its point of rest at the bottom and turns three quarters of a circle and stops at right angles to a vertical line drawn through the center of the balance. The force of the spring will encounter a resistance due to gravity acting on the weight as it starts upward toward the top, and after reaching the top and starting downward, the force of gravity is an added force downward. The effect would be a retardation during the first portion of the path and an acceleration during the latter portion to the extent that, for arcs *above* approximately 450 degrees the watch will lose   It would seem, therefore, that at some point near to 450 degrees these forces would counteract each other.   Some authorities place this figure at 444 degrees.

Poising the balance. Place the balance on a poising tool and start the balance in motion. During the time it is rotating hold a small compass as near as possible to the circumference of the balance so as to ascertain whether or not it is magnetized.   It is useless to attempt to poise a magnetized balance; hence the first act is to demagnetize it if it shows even the slightest bit of magnetism

The balance having been demagnetized and found satisfactory, proceed with the poising Having located the position of the heavy point it is good practice to take note of the position of the regulator   This is our guide in deciding whether we should reduce the weight at the heavy point or add weight opposite to the heavy point, thus saving a certain amount of timing after the watch is again running.

Should we find, when altering the weights, that the heavy point has shifted a short distance we may feel certain that good progress is being made. However, if it is found that the heavy point has been shifted to the opposite side it is evident that the correction has been overdone. It follows, therefore, that in altering the weights we should proceed with caution and thereby save much time, besides realizing a much better piece of work.

Parallel pliers with cardboard glued to the jaws are very effective for holding the balance while removing and replacing the screws.

MAGNETISM

Magnetism is an ever-constant and insidious enemy to horologists. The means by which a watch may be magnetized are so numerous today that it is important that the repairman form the habit of testing every watch for magnetism that comes in for regulation, examination or repair.

In testing for magnetism place a small compass not only over the balance but also over the winding wheels. The mainspring being subject to magnetization as well as other steel parts, has definite poles at the time the magnetic lines of force passes through the watch. These poles are split up into countless numbers as the mainspring unwinds. This constant alteration of the relative position of the poles between the mainspring, winding wheels, and the balance helps to explain the erratic performance of magnetized watches.

Theory of demagnetization. An alternating current is that type of electrical current that changes its direction constantly and when such current flows through a coil of wire the poles also change. Figure 2 shows a conception of an alternating current wave as it moves through *time,* and the complete wave is called a cycle. An alternating current of 60 such waves per second is said to have a frequency of 60 cycles.

When a steel rod is inserted in a demagnetizer and the flow of alternating current is suddenly cut off, the steel rod will be found to be magnetized, its poles being that of the last half cycle that was sent through the wire. However, if the current is left on and the rod gradually withdrawn, the result will be different. It will be repolarized for every cycle and each successive polarization will be weaker than

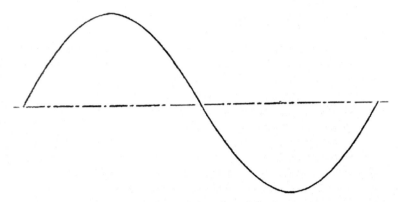

Figure 2.   Wave form of alternating current.

the preceding one.   When withdrawn entirely from the field,
the magnetism has disappeared.

Demagnetizing a watch. The procedure in demagnetizing
a watch is much the same as explained above.   Withdraw
the watch, keeping it central with the opening and giving it
a slight twist after leaving the opening. Continue the with-
drawal until the watch is about three feet or more from the
demagnetizer.   If the first attempt fails to remove all magnetism repeat the operation.

Magnetized tools. The horologists' tools are subject to
being magnetized.   Screw drivers and tweezers should be
closely watched. Avoid placing such tools in a north-south
position in or on the bench.

Problems

1.   Why should balance pivots be made perfectly round?
2.   What is the effect of giving impulse to the balance or pendulum before the point of rest? after the point of rest?

3 What is the effect of the lever escapement on the position rating of a watch?

4 Is the counterpoise on the pallet fork of very great importance?

5. Does the type of fastening on the outer end of the mainspring have anything to do with the friction between the coils?

6. What is the proper arc of motion of the balance?

7. How do you ascertain the correct arc of motion?

8. What is the most common cause of position error?

9. If the excess of weight is on the lower side of the balance when at rest, will the watch gain or lose when running at an arc of 540 degrees? when running at an arc of 350 degrees?

10 What balance arc is considered the neutral arc?

11. How do you go about poising the balance?

12. How do you demagnetize a watch?

CHAPTER TWO

Position Adjusting

THE FIRST portion of this chapter treats on position error as related solely to the balance spring and of the effect of gravity which is an ever-present force acting upon the innermost coils. The nature of this action is such that a positive position error is produced.

A watch may be mechanically perfect—that is, its construction from barrel to balance may be as exact as human skill knows how to make it—and yet, in spite of such perfection, there will be a variation of from 15 to 30 seconds in 24 hours between some two vertical positions due to the condition of the balance spring alone. In watches that are less perfect the error is frequently as high as 40 seconds or more.

The Balance Spring and Its Poise Error

The oscillation of the inner portion of the spring corresponds very nearly to that of the collet; that is, when the collet travels three fourths of a circle, the first coil in the center travels nearly an equal distance. It is further evident that each of the several coils, as they tend to become more distant from the center, will travel a shorter path until the movement ceases altogether at the regulator pins. If the coils are marked in a straight line from collet to regulator

140

pins, one would readily observe the distance traveled by the several coils and the extent of their path under different arcs of motion.

It is impossible to poise a spiral spring. Therefore it is at once evident that it is the oscillation of the unpoised inner portion of the spring, when acted upon by the pull of gravity, that causes position error in the vertical positions. A statement as to how this works need not be repeated here, for the analysis given in the preceding chapter relative to the poise error of the balance, applies to this condition also. However, slightly varied effects under different arcs of motion result, due to the fact that the greater mass of the unpoised inner portion of the spring vibrates in a shorter arc than does the balance proper.

Experimental demonstration. A demonstration at the command of every horologist is to take several watches and run them, first with the figure 1 up, and following with the figures 2, 3, 4, etc., continuing the experiment around the dial with all figures up, running the watches in each of the 12 positions for 24 hours and taking note of the rate in each position. If an electric timing machine is available the experiment can be made most conveniently and in a very short time.

Table 1 shows the result of an experiment as stated above, using four popular makes of American watches All watches were in excellent condition with balances perfectly poised, fitted with theoretically corrected overcoils, and the grades ranged from 17 jewels to 21 jewels. The arc of motion of the balance of all watches was about 540 degrees when fully wound and more than 450 degrees after 24 hours of running

In watch Number 1 the rate was fastest at the time when

the figure 11 was up; in watch Number 2 the rate was fastest
at the time when the figure 3 was up. The watches Number
3 and Number 4 had definite fast positions also, and in all
watches the slow position was opposite or nearly opposite that
of the fast position.

TABLE 1

	NO. 1 Secs	NO. 2 Secs	NO. 3 Secs	NO. 4 Secs.
1	0	+ 4	+ 1	+ 3
2	— 4	+ 5	+ 1	0
3	— 6	+ 8	— 3	— 2
4	— 8	+ 3	— 3	— 5
5	—11	0	— 7	— 7
6	—10	— 2	— 5	— 8
7	— 5	— 6	+ 1	0
8	— 1	—10	+ 2	+ 1
9	— 2	—12	+ 2	+ 5
10	0	— 3	+ 3	+ 5
11	+ 4	0	+ 5	+ 6
12	0	+ 3	+ 4	+ 8

THE NATURAL ERROR AND METHODS OF CORRECTION

An examination of the balance spring showed that the
fastest rate always occurred at the time when the middle of
the first half of the innermost coil happened to be up This
error, due to the oscillation of the center of gravity of the
inner portion of the spring, is called the natural error and
is unavoidable. We can, however, make such alterations so
as to limit the fullest manifestation of the error in three
ways These are as follows:

*1. Pin the spring at the collet in such a position that the
natural error will be the least detrimental to the uniform
rate of the watch*

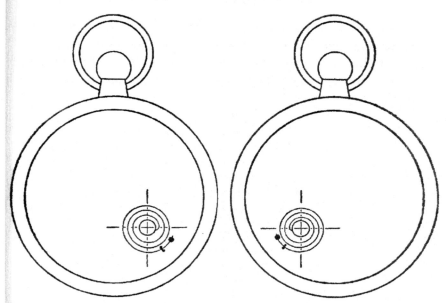

Figure 3. Proper pinning at the collet. Figure 4. Proper pinning at the collet.

2. Reduce the natural error by the application o, correct terminal curves both outside and inside.

3. Neutralize the effect of the natural error by counter-poising the balance.

These corrections will now be considered in the order stated above.

The proper pinning at the collet. When fitting new balance springs to pocket watches, certain pinning points should be observed if the best position rates are to be expected. The proper pinning at the collet is shown in Figures 3 and 4. The first half of the innermost coil tends upward as it leaves the collet in the direction of pendant up, producing a fast pendant-up rate. It does not matter if the spring tends to the left as shown in Figure 3 or tends to the right as shown in Figure 4, for it can be readily seen that, in either case, the middle of the first half of the innermost coil stands in the direction of pendant up. When the spring is pinned as stated above, the pendant-right and pendant-left positions will have a slower but a nearly equal rate, provided the balance spring is properly centered and vibrates concentrically. The greater part of the natural error will show up only in the pendant-down position, and since a pocket watch in practical usage is seldom if ever subjected to this position, it follows naturally that the pendant-down error is of little importance.

Reducing the natural error. It was stated in the first portion of this chapter that finely constructed watches vary from 15 to 30 seconds in 24 hours between some two vertical positions and watches that are less perfect would vary as much as 40 seconds and more. If the natural error is shown to be more than 30 seconds in 24 hours, the excessive variation is due to want of perfection of the inner terminal of the spring. A slight eccentric motion at the inner terminal will cause a greater variation than would be the case if the spring were perfectly true. Thus it is clear that the balance spring should always be faultlessly trued at the collet and equal attention should be given to both the flat and the round.

The Breguet type balance spring on position error. It would now be natural for one to inquire as to the effect of the Breguet spring with correct terminal as compared with the ordinary flat spring on position error. Experiments have demonstrated that the Breguet spring does reduce the variation in the vertical positions, but only to a small degree, proving that the position error is due primarily to the oscillation of the center of gravity of the inner portion of the spring.

Table 2 shows the results of an experiment using both the flat and Breguet springs. The watch selected for this example was an 18 size, 15-jewel grade, fitted with a flat spring. The first column of the table shows the rate with the flat spring, and the second column shows the rate with the same spring after it was made over into a Breguet with correct terminal. The watch was run in each position for 24 hours.

TABLE 2

	FLAT SPRING *Secs.*	BREGUET SPRING *Secs*
Pendant up	+ 7	+ 7
Pendant right	+ 5	+ 3
Pendant left	— 6	— 2
Pendant down	— 8	—10

Counterpoising the balance. If the most perfect terminal curves do not produce the desired results, counterpoising may be tried A general rule for the alteration is as follows: *Reduce the weight on the lower side of the balance in the position that is slow.* It is assumed that the balance has a good motion and that at no time does the arc of motion fall below 450 degrees during the 24 hours that the watch is under observation. This is important if success in counterpoising is to be expected. It should further be understood that any alteration of the poise should be practiced only to a limited extent; otherwise, a most unsatisfactory and erratic rate will result. Usually just a slight touch of the poising saw will reduce the natural error as much as 5 to 10 seconds in 24 hours.

Use of the Regulator Pins in Adjusting

The condition of the regulator pins play an important part in the position rating of a watch. In fact, by slightly opening or closing the pins as the case may require, it is possible to bring the horizontal and vertical positions in close agreement.

Let us suppose, for example, that the regulator pins are opened slightly and the first coil of the spring vibrates equally between the pins. We have literally made the active length of the spring longer and the watch will go slower. It also changes the rate between the long and short arcs. The effect can be explained in this way:

Suppose that the balance is vibrating at an arc of 180 degrees and the first coil of the spring barely touches the pins. For arcs below 180 degrees, the active length of the spring will commence very nearly from the stud. Now, if the arc of motion is increased to 540 degrees, the active length of the spring will be shortened, commencing more nearly from the pins. This will make the long arcs go faster and the effect will vary in proportion to the changes taking place in the arc of motion.

Suppose now that the pins are open, but instead of the first coil of the spring vibrating equally between them, the first coil leans against one of the pins. Assume that it requires an arc of 360 degrees to lift the coil away from the pin against which it leans It is plain that for arcs below 360 degrees the active length of the spring will commence from the pins, and for arcs above 360 degrees the active length will commence more nearly from the stud. This condition will make the long arcs go slower, or, in other words, opposite to that in the former instance. Thus it can be seen that the condition of the regulator pins may be the cause of many of the disorders in the performance of watches. It is also true that an intelligent manipulation of the pins is the quickest and simplest means of correcting the variation in the rate between the horizontal and vertical positions because of the fact that the arc of motion is always shorter in the vertical positions. The practical use of the regulator pins is stated in the following rules ·

1. If the regulator pins are closed and the watch gains in the pendant-up position, a slower pendant-up rate is obtained by opening the pins.

2. If the regulator pins are open and the watch loses in the pendant-up position, a faster pendant-up rate is obtained by closing the pins.

The spring should be so adjusted that the vibration of the coil between the pins is equal; otherwise, the coil will strike one pin with more force than the other, and the result will be very different from that stated in the above rules. Also in spreading the pins, the vibration of the coil between them should be very slight and discernible only with a powerful glass. The pins should never be spread more than enough to slow the mean rate 3 seconds an hour. If spread beyond that amount the watch is apt to become a very unreliable timepiece; in other words, position adjusting by the manipulation of the regulator pins can be practiced only to a limited extent.

Adjustment to the Horizontal Positions

Effect of manipulating the regulator pins on the horizontal positions. We have seen that the rates between dial up and pendant up can be equalized by the manipulation of the regulator pins. Should we alter the pins to secure the desired results between dial up and pendant up, we could expect a change in the rate between the horizontal positions also. Often the horizontal rates are improved; sometimes they are reversed. This would suggest that the adjustment to the horizontal positions should be made last—that is, after the corrections for dial up and pendant up are satisfactory

After a little reflection it is evident that the difference in the rate is due to the anisochronism of the balance spring. The manipulation of the pins not only corrects the rate between dial up and pendant up, but more often than otherwise it improves the isochronal rate also. This can be shown by running a given watch in the position of dial up for 8 hours at an arc of 540 degrees and taking note of the rate and then running it again for another 8 hours at an arc of 360 degrees. If the rate is slower when running at 360 degrees the pendant-up rate will usually be slower *Occasionally there are exceptions.*

Correction of errors in the horizontal positions. Errors between the horizontal positions come generally under the head of frictional errors and have to do with changes in the arc of motion of the balance. A variation of 2, 3, or even 4 seconds is unimportant. Extreme variation can be laid to rough pivots, dirt or thick oil, hole jewels that are too small or too large, pitted cap jewels, balance pivots not the same size, or a balance spring out of flat. As a rule the fast position takes the shorter arc, which would suggest that the position producing the fast rate is the one that calls for correction. Assuming that the staff and jewels are as nearly perfect as an inspection with a strong glass can determine, a general rule for the correction of the rate in the horizontal positions reads as follows: *Round slightly the lower pivot in the position that is fast.*

Problems

1 Is it possible to poise perfectly a balance spring?

2 What is the natural error? In what manner does it affect the position rating of a watch?

3 What is the proper pinning at the collet?

4. Does the outer terminal of the balance spring have a greater or smaller effect on the position rating of a watch as compared with the inner terminal?

5. Can the regulator pins be of use in adjusting a watch to position? Explain.

6. What are the usual causes of position error in the horizontal positions?

CHAPTER THREE

Adjustment to Isochronism

THE ADJUSTMENT to isochronism is that adjustment which has to do with the maintaining of a constant rate over a definite period of time. Absolute isochronism is impossible to attain because of several factors which are inherent in the balance spring and for which there are no practical remedies.

A pendulum will make the long and short vibrations in equal time. Start a pendulum in motion, traveling over a given space in a given time. As the motion falls off, it will be observed that the time consumed in each vibration does not change. A slower or faster rate can be produced only by lengthening or shortening the pendulum. The pendulum is in reality a falling body and the laws which apply to falling bodies apply to the pendulum also. Therefore adding or reducing the weight of the pendulum does not affect the time of vibration, for any change made in the mass carries with it a proportional force in that of gravity.

Adding to or reducing the mass of the balance varies the rate of vibration, for the strength of the balance spring does not change. There are three factors upon which the time of the vibration of the balance depends. They are:

1. The weight of the balance.
2. The diameter of the balance.

3. The strength of the balance spring.

As already stated, the balance spring is the cause of the more important disturbing factors in the isochronal rating of watches. Of these disturbing factors, our attention will first be directed to the problem of isochronism as affected by varying the total length of the spring.

The Length of the Balance Spring on Isochronism

In every balance spring there is a certain length in which the long and short vibrations are practically isochronal. *Now if this length is ascertained and we make the spring shorter by whole coils, the short arcs will go faster; and if we make the spring longer by whole coils, the short arcs will go slower.*

It will be observed that the shortening or lengthening is done only by whole coils. The reason for this is explained in the following statement. If the spring is shortened by some portion of a coil and not by whole coils, another effect would take place which would alter the isochronism. For example, the shortening of the spring by one half of a coil may cause the short arcs to produce a losing rate instead of a gaining rate. This problem is one that is distinctly separate from the one now under discussion and it will be treated more in detail in the next section.

A spring that is practically isochronal as far as the length is concerned usually consists of about 13 coils. Springs supplied by the manufacturer are correct for length. The thought to remember from that which has been stated above is that in fitting a new spring, the spring should not be shortened excessively in timing, for in so doing the isochronal rate is affected

The Flat and Breguet Balance Spring
on Isochronism

The flat spring. If one will examine a flat spring in a watch during the time the balance is in motion, it will be observed that the vibration is wholly on one side and on the side opposite the regulator pins. This is not all the eccentric motion present in the spring, however, for a similar motion takes place opposite the inner terminal, although it is less visible to the eye These eccentric motions affect the isochronism because of several conditions. The principal ones are: (1) a constant oscillation of the center of gravity, (2) a persistent pushing and pulling at the balance pivots, and (3) the effect of torsion, with which this section is particularly concerned

Action of the flat balance spring. Torsion is a circular impulse which takes place at the innermost coils of the spring. The result is a retardation or an acceleration, depending on the relative positions of the two eccentric motions as the balance vibrates. The anisochronism thus produced can be varied by altering the length of the spring. Such alterations, of course, change the angular distance between the inner terminal and the regulator pins, and it is this change of angular distance that decides the rate between the long and the short arcs. The laws governing the isochronism as concerned with the above statement are as follows.

1. When the angular distance between the inner terminal and the regulator pins stands at even coils, that is, whole coils, the short arcs gain.

2. When the angular distance between the inner terminal and the regulator pins stands at even coils, plus half a coil, the short arcs lose.

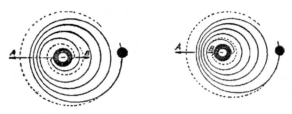

Figure 5.   Figure 6.

3. When the angular distance between the inner terminal and the regulator pins stands at even coils plus one fourth or three fourths of a coil, the long and short arcs are more nearly isochronal.

Let us assume that the arc of motion of a given balance is 360 degrees, as an example of a short arc. If the spring is pinned at even coils, the eccentric motions will stand in opposite directions. According to rule 1, this produces a gaining rate as compared with the long arcs. This can be explained by reason of the fact that the eccentric motion of the outermost coils exerts a force (when wound up) in the direction of the arrow A, Figure 5, while the eccentric motion of the innermost coil exerts a force in the direction of the arrow B, and since these forces are in opposite directions, there is a tendency toward acceleration as the arcs become shorter than 540 degrees and the maximum is reached at 360 degrees. In unwinding, the forces are reversed but their relation to each other is the same.

If the spring is pinned at even coils plus half a coil, the eccentric motions will stand in the same direction, namely: opposite the regulator pins. According to rule 2, this produces a losing rate as compared with the long arcs. Since the forces of the eccentric motions are in the same direction,

Figure 6, there is less resistance or divergence of forces and the balance may vibrate a little farther, hence a retardation takes place

If the spring is pinned at even coils plus one fourth or three fourths of a coil, the eccentric motions will stand at right angles to each other, the effects stated in rules 1 and 2 will be neutralized, and the watch will function at a more nearly isochronal rate. Of course, when the watch is put to practical usage, the motion of the balance is constantly changing and this fact considerably complicates results.

The effect of torsion should not be confused with that of the oscillation of the center of gravity, for the latter is a function that is distinctly different and plays only a small part in producing an anisochronism. The effect of torsion is by far the most disturbing element and the only way its effect may be reduced, aside from varying the terminal pinnings, is the application of the most perfect terminal curves, both outside and inside.

Reducing the isochronal error. The superior performance of the Breguet spring in the attainment of isochronism is the reason for the passing of the flat spring. The above analysis of the flat spring would at once suggest that it is possible to vary the isochronism by manipulating the overcoil of the Breguet spring so as to throw the eccentric motion in some desired direction. That is correct reasoning; however, a spring that produces concentric vibrations will attain close enough isochronism in most watches while at the same time realizing the best position rating in the vertical positions.

Modern watches are built with a better design and proportion of parts than the older models and the correction of isochronism by means of altering a correct terminal is seldom necessary However, if the most perfect terminal curves do not produce the desired results, the following rules for altering the overcoil may be used.

1. If the short arcs are slow, bring in part of the body of the spring and add it to the overcoil.

2 If the short arcs are fast, take part of the overcoil and move it back into the body of the spring.

Problems

1 What is the effect of shortening a balance spring by whole coils on the isochronal rating of a watch?

2. What is torsion? What are the effects on a flat balance spring?

3 In what manner do you alter the overcoil to accelerate the short arcs?

4. In what manner do you alter the overcoil to retard the short arcs?

CHAPTER FOUR

The Adjustment to Temperature

IN ORDER to attain a practical system for the temperature adjustment, the general practice has been to solder together brass and steel for the rim of the balance. The brass occupies the outer portion of the rim, consuming about three fifths of the total thickness. The rim is cut near the arms to permit the turning in and out of the loose ends, thus changing the active diameter of the wheel. This movement compensates for the changing elasticity of the balance spring during temperature changes. This type of balance is known as the compensating balance. A compensating balance made of brass and Invar (a nickle-and-steel alloy) when used in connection with a hardened steel balance spring has been and is today the most satisfactory arrangement for combating the temperature error.

However, there is a definite trend toward the use of a plain uncut balance of a single metal and a balance spring of a nonrusting, nonmagnetizing alloy, made principally of iron, nickle, chromium, and tungsten, called Elinvar. A slight temperature error exists, but there are certain advantages that make it desirable to continue research for further improvement. This is apparently the opinion of watch factories, for new models have appeared lately with definite changes in the design of the movement as well as the balance and spring, showing a persistent effort on the part of manufacturers to improve this new type of balance assembly.

Correcting the temperature error. Watches with compensating balances are usually adjusted to temperature between 40 degrees Fahrenheit and 95 degrees Fahrenheit. The rules for the adjustment are as follows:

1. If the watch runs slow in heat, move any even number of screws that are opposite each other an equal distance toward the loose ends of the rims.

2. If the watch runs fast in heat, move any even number of screws that are opposite each other an equal distance toward the balance arms.

Experience in effecting temperature adjustment is necessary before the horologist is able to decide on the extent of the alterations. More often than otherwise, several trials are required. If the screws are moved considerable distance the poise should be examined. Temperature adjustment is practically permanent. The balance may be trued and poised many times without interfering with the temperature adjustment. However, in changing a balance spring, readjustment would be necessary.

Equipment used for temperature adjusting. The equipment used for temperature adjusting is an oven and a refrigerator. An oven suitable for the purpose need be nothing more than a box fitted with an electric light bulb, a rheostat, and a thermometer The thermometer is placed inside and in such a manner that it can be conveniently read through an opening in the box. An ordinary electric refrigerator will serve the purpose for the lower temperature.

Problems

1. Does the fitting of a new balance spring alter the temperature adjustment of a watch?

2   A watch that is equipped with a compensating balance runs slow in heat. How do you correct the error?

3   Name the advantages of a solid, single-metal balance and Elinvar balance spring.

CHAPTER FIVE

The Practical Work of Adjusting

THE PRACTICAL use of the instruction that has been written in these pages will presently be demonstrated by several examples taken from actual practice when the writer was engaged in practical work at the bench. The data for the watches to be adjusted are kept in a small notebook. The date, customer's name, the make, size and grade of the watch are recorded, followed by the several rates and an account of the changes made to effect a satisfactory rating.

Practical Problems in the Adjustment to Positions

Preliminary notes. It will be necessary to briefly discuss several factors before considering the concrete problems. The method of computing the variation of the rate in the different positions will be next in order and to assist in the explanation, the reader is referred to Adjustment 4 on page 163. The first column, reading down, shows the progressive rate—that is, the rate without setting the watch except at the beginning of the test. The first figure shows a loss of 2 seconds, the rate for 24 hours, written —2, the rate for dial up. Without setting the watch, the figure below shows the variation after running the watch in the position of dial down, which is +2. The next figure below shows the variation after running in the position of pendant up, the rate being —19. For pendant right the progressive rate is —30 and for pendant left the progressive rate is —43.

The rate for each period of 24 hours is computed by subtracting the lesser figure from the greater, provided the rates are all plus or all minus. However, if the rates are plus and minus, the figures are added and the sign before the last rate added is prefixed to the 24-hour rate and entered in the second column. To make this clear, we shall continue with the example, explaining it in this way: The rate for dial up, recorded as —2, is carried to the second column The rate for dial down is computed by adding together —2 and +2 and the rate is entered in the second column as +4, showing the amount of the gain in excess of correct time. The rate for pendant up is computed by adding together +2 and —19, and the result is entered in the second column as —21, showing the amount of loss deducted from correct time. The rate for pendant right is the difference between —19 and —30 and the rate for pendant left is the difference between —30 and —43, both of which are shown in the second column. Thus we may compute the 24-hour rate without the necessity of setting the watch for every trial. Of course, this is not necessary when the electric timing machine is used

Maximum allowance in positions. Before testing in positions the watch should be regulated to run within 15 seconds in 24 hours The extent of variation between 5 positions in high-grade, 16-size watches should not exceed 6 seconds in 24 hours. For watches of a cheaper grade and for most of the average grades in the 12 size, a variation of not more than 10 seconds is considered passable. The rate between the positions of dial up and pendant up are the most important and should receive special consideration. The rate between these two positions should not exceed 3 or 4 seconds; in fact, it is not difficult to produce close agreement and in most cases the manipulation of the regulator is all that is necessary.

In the following pages are shown several examples of 3 and 5 position adjusting. These examples should be studied carefully.

Adjustment 1.

Watch—16 size, 23 jewels

Repairs—cleaned, staff fitted, balance poised.

After cleaning and repairing, the watch was tested in 3 positions and it was found to have a variation of 15 seconds with a gain in the pendant-up position.

Dial up   — 6   —6
Dial down   —12   —6
Pendant up   — 3   +9   (15)

An examination showed that the spring was level and properly centered and that the regulator pins were tightly closed Accordingly the pins were spread slightly and after timing by turning in a pair of timing screws, the test was again tried, this time with the following results.

Dial up   —2   —2
Dial down   —5   —3
Pendant up   —9   —4   (2)

Adjustment 2.

Watch—16 size, 7 jewels

Repairs—Cleaned, main spring fitted

The first test showed a variation of 28 seconds as shown below.

Dial up $+ 8$ $+ 8$
Dial down $+15$ $+ 7$
Pendant up $+48$ $+33$ (28)

The error being considerable in the pendant-up position, it was reasoned that the balance was out of poise The spring was removed and the balance was tested for poise. A slight poise error was found, but the want of poise could not be responsible for the whole variation of 28 seconds. Therefore in addition to poising the balance, the regulator pins were spread slightly and after timing the watch, the next test showed a much improved rate.

Dial up $+3$ $+3$
Dial down $+6$ $+3$
Pendant up $+5$ -1 (4)

Adjustment 3.

Watch—16 size, 17 jewels

Repairs—cleaned, balance poised

This example showed a loss in the pendant-up position instead of a gain as found in the previous examples

Dial up $- 2$ $- 2$
Dial down $- 4$ $- 2$
Pendant up -18 -14 (12)

As the watch was in excellent condition throughout, the error was most likely to be found in the regulator pins. An examination showed that the pins were open and the correction consisted of closing the pins. A much improved rate is shown on the second test

Dial up -1 -1
Dial down -2 -1
Pendant up -5 -3 (2)

The adjustment to five positions consists in running the watch in the positions of pendant right and pendant left in addition to dial up, dial down, and pendant up. Because you find a close rate between the three positions is no proof that the watch will be an excellent timepiece. Errors could be present that would show up only in the pendant-right and pendant-left positions Fine watches should be adjusted to five positions, for often an unsuspected error in the general construction of the watch is discovered.

Adjustment 4.
  Watch—18 size, 15 jewels
  Repairs—cleaned

The first test showed the following rate.

Dial up	— 2	— 2	
Dial down	+ 2	+ 4	
Pendant up	—19	—21	
Pendant right	—30	—11	
Pendant left	—43	—13	(25)

The balance spring was pinned so that the fast position stood in the direction of pendant up, yet the pendant-up rate was slow The dial-up and dial-down rates were also too great to be allowed to pass.

The balance was placed in the truing calipers and the balance spring was examined and found to have an eccentric motion at the collet. (Incidentally, the spring was removed and the balance was tested for poise, showing a slight poise error with the excess of weight on the lower side of the balance when in the pendant-up position) The balance was poised and the balance spring replaced and trued Further examination showed a slight vibration of the spring between the regulator pins. Since the rates in the vertical positions were all slow the pins were closed. The watch was regulated to mean time and the results of the second test are shown as follows.

Dial up	— 2	—2
Dial down	— 3	—1
Pendant up	— 7	—4
Pendant right	—12	—5
Pendant left	—20	—8

(7)

Adjustment 5.

Watch—16 size, 21 jewels

Repairs—cleaned, staff fitted, balance poised

The horologist should be cautioned that there will be frequently found watches that do not function satisfactorily in position even though the balance and spring and the general construction seem perfect in every detail. As already stated, the watch must be mechanically in good order and it is possible that some mechanical detail has been overlooked. The example below was selected to show that the general condition of the watch was responsible for the error in position.

Dial up	— 2	— 2
Dial down	+ 6	+ 8
Pendant up	+ 7	+ 1
Pendant right	+17	+10
Pendant left	—10	—27

(37)

The first test, as shown above, was far from satisfactory. This condition could not be due to want of adjustment of the balance and spring as the balance was poised and the spring was properly fitted, with the regulator pins closed.

The arc of motion of the balance was examined and found to be somewhat shorter than it should be. Since the escapement was in excellent condition, it was assumed that the main spring was set, and an examination showed that such was the case. A new spring was fitted and the motion was considerably improved. The train was examined and a cracked jewel in the pallet bridge was discovered, although the crack was so slight that it was discernible only with a strong glass. A new jewel was fitted and without doing anything else the next test showed a much improved rate.

Dial up	+2	+2
Dial down	+3	+1
Pendant up	—1	—4
Pendant right	—1	0
Pendant left	—7	—6 (8)

Adjustment 6.

Watch—12 size, 17 jewels

Repairs—cleaned, balance poised, balance spring trued

This example shows that it is possible to have a close rate between the horizontal positions and pendant up, yet the pendant-right and pendant-left positions may be far from satisfactory

Dial up	— 5	— 5
Dial down	— 4	+ 1
Pendant up	— 3	+ 1
Pendant right	—23	—20
Pendant left	—98	—75 (76)

The watch showed an abnormally slow rate in the pendant-left position. It was observed that the arc of motion of the

balance was shorter than it should be. Further examination
showed that the drop locks were too deep, and, accordingly,
the drop locks were made lighter The escapement was re-
banked to the drop and the necessary corrections made, yet
after the balance was replaced the arc of motion was still too
short. The mainspring was removed and found to be somewhat set and a little weaker than should be used in this grade
of watch. After replacing the mainspring with one of the
proper strength, the next test in position showed the following results .

Dial up	— 4	—4
Dial down	— 5	—1
Pendant up	— 5	0
Pendant right	—11	—6
Pendant left	—18	—7 (7)

Adjustment 7.

Watch—16 size, 23 jewels

Repairs—cleaned, staff fitted, balance poised.

The first test in positions showed the following rate:

Dial up	0	0
Dial down	— 1	— 1
Pendant up	+ 4	+ 5
Pendant right	+17	+13
Pendant left	+13	— 4 (17)

The watch having a fairly satisfactory rate except for the
pendant-right position, it was reasoned that a slight counterpoise would correct the error. Accordingly, the screw on the
lower side of the balance in the position that was slow, namely
pendant left, was reduced very slightly. The next test showed
the following results:

Dial up	0	0
Dial down	—2	—2
Pendant up	0	+2
Pendant right	+3	+3
Pendant left	+5	+2 (5)

It will be observed that the counterpoise retarded the fast position more than it accelerated the slow position. This is always the case. The excess of weight, when placed below the center of gravity, will retard the rate more than the same weight, when placed above, will accelerate the rate. This is a point to remember when attempting the correction of a position error by counterpoising.

Adjustment 8.

Watch—12 size, 17 jewels

Repairs—cleaned, balance poised, new balance spring
        fitted

In this example the balance spring was selected from a stock of uncolleted springs. The spring was vibrated. colleted and trued at the collet, overcoil formed, and corrected to produce concentric vibrations. The first test showed the following rate.

Dial up	+ 5	+ 5
Dial down	— 5	—10
Pendant up	+12	+17
Pendant right	+22	+10
Pendant left	+34	+12
Pendant down	+19	—15 (32)

The natural error being considerable, it was decided that a new inner terminal should be made About three inner coils were broken out and the Lossier inner terminal was formed. Noting also that the dial-up position was fast the lower pivot was rounded slightly After timing the watch, the second test showed the following rate.

Dial up	0	0	Pendant right	— 5	— 5
Dial down	0	0	Pendant left	— 8	— 3
Pendant up	0	0	Pendant down	—18	—10 (10)

This example with the Lossier inner curve is given to show how the natural error can be reduced. The very best rates can be attained only with poised collets and theoretical inner terminals. The above watch when carried by the owner performed at a rate within ten seconds a month.

Practical Problem in Isochronal Adjusting

In the chronometer it is possible to attain isochronism by altering the form of the terminal curves or by selecting a certain relation of the pinnings between collet and stud However, any attempt made to effect isochronism by these methods in watches may seriously interfere with the position adjustment. As the position adjustment is more important, it is desirable to sacrifice the isochronal rating when both cannot be satisfied. If the spring is pinned correctly for position adjustment, the best pinning for isochronism may or may not exist, depending on the length of the spring and the design of the watch As stated in Chapter Three, Isochronal Adjusting, the best we can do to attain practical isochronism in watches lies in the correct formation of the terminal curves.

Balance springs supplied by the manufacturer. When fitting a spring supplied by the manufacturer for a certain model of watch the proper length need not be considered, for that factor has already been taken care of by the maker. There are occasions, however, when the spring in the watch has been considerably shortened by some workman who was not acquainted with the laws of isochronism as governed by the length of the spring. In such cases the spring must be replaced with a new one of the proper length, if practical isochronism is to be expected.

Method used in testing isochronism. After being wound and set, the watch is run for 6 hours, after which time the rate is recorded. The watch is then run for 24 hours from the time it was wound and set, when rate is again recorded. The watch is run 6 hours longer without winding and the rate is recorded for the third time. The rate for the first and last period of 6 hours is separately computed for a period of 24 hours. In this manner the variation of the rate is shown for the long and short arcs.

A practical problem. In showing an example of isochronal adjusting it is possible only to prove that which has already been stated. The following example, therefore, shows how the correction of the eccentric motion of the balance spring improves the isochronism. The spring had an eccentric motion in the direction opposite the regulator pins and the first test showed the following results:

Long arcs	2:00 P.M. set	0
	8:00 P.M	—1
	Rate in 24 hours	—4
Short arcs	2:00 P.M. next day	—3
	8:00 P M.	—7
	Rate in 24 hours	—16 (12)

The first test showed a loss of 12 seconds in the short arcs.

After correcting the overcoil so that the vibrations of the spring were concentric to the center of the balance, the next test showed a much improved rate.

Long arcs
$\begin{cases} \text{9 00 A.M. set} & 0 \\ \text{3 :00 P.M.} & 0 \\ \text{Rate in 24 hours} & 0 \end{cases}$

Short arcs
$\begin{cases} \text{9 :00 A.M. next day} & +1 \\ \text{3 .00 P.M.} & +\frac{1}{2} \\ \text{Rate in 24 hours} & -2 \quad (2) \end{cases}$

Practical Problem in Temperature Adjusting

Of all the adjustments of watches temperature adjustment is the best understood, no doubt because of the fact that it has been the principal error to be eradicated in the chronometer and therefore studied more than the other.

One example of temperature adjusting will suffice, as the correction in all cases consists merely of moving opposite pairs of balance screws from one position to another.

The example shown below had a rate of 20 seconds fast in heat:

Cold —5   Heat +15

To show the location of the screws and the position to which they are moved, it is customary to number the screw holes The holes nearest the arms are numbered *1*, the next *2*, the next *3*, etc , the highest number indicating the last holes near the loose ends of the rims.

Since this example showed a gain in heat, the correction consisted of moving the screws at the free ends of the rims toward the balance arm. Accordingly, the screws in holes number *9* were moved to holes number *5*, and the screws in holes number *11* were moved to holes number *9*. The next test showed a variation of 10 seconds slow in heat.

Cold +10   Heat   0

This shows that the correction was overdone. Therefore the screws in holes number *9* were moved to holes number *11*. The next test as recorded below shows a very satisfactory rate.

Cold +6   Heat +5

Final Timing and Regulating

Timing screws and washers. After a watch has been cleaned and repaired, the variation in time should not be corrected by moving the regulator, but rather by turning in or out the timing screws as the watch may require. Some watches do not have timing screws and the correction must necessarily consist in undercutting the balance screws or adding timing washers. If the watch runs within 30 seconds in 24 hours the regulator may be used.

The middle temperature error. It was stated in Chapter Four of Part I that the middle temperature error causes a variation of from 2 to 6 seconds, being faster than the rates between the extremes of heat and cold. It is better, therefore, to regulate the watches on the rack to run a few seconds fast rather than just on time, for the watches on the rack are running in the normal temperature and the middle temperature errort is in effect. When carried in the pocket the higher temperature would cause the watch to run slow.

Delivering the watch. When delivering a watch to the customer tell him that it is preferable to wind the watch in the morning. There is a good reason for so doing. The best part of the mainspring is used during the day when the watch is carried. Since the balance has a slightly shorter arc of motion when running in a vertical position, it is better to take advantage of the extra power that would be avalable by winding in the morning. Because a watch is usually laid flat on a table or dresser at night it is at once evident that a more nearly uniform balance arc takes place if the above practice of winding the watch is adhered to.

The horologist should take time to explain to the customer that there will probably be a variation of several seconds during the first few weeks of carrying the watch and ask the party to come in, in a week or two, for comparison with the correct time and for further regulation if necessary. Tell the customer that it takes several weeks to properly regulate a watch and that he may come in as often as he finds it convenient. In this manner much of the dissatisfaction of the repair department is eliminated besides making many friends for the store.

GLOSSARY OF TERMS

Addendum. The portion of a tooth of a wheel or pinion beyond the pitch circle.

Arbor. Axis of the balance wheel or mainspring barrel.

Balance. The vibrating wheel of a watch, which, in conjunction with the balance spring, regulates the progress of the hands.

Balance arc. A part of the vibration of a balance.

Balance cock. The support for the upper pivot of the balance staff.

Balance spring. A long fine spring that regulates the vibration of the balance.

Balance staff. The axis of the balance.

Banking pins. Two pins that limit the angular motion of the lever.

Banking to the drop. An adjustment of the banking pins permitting the escape wheel teeth to drop off the pallets.

Barrel. A circular box for the reception of the mainspring.

Barrel arbor. The axis of the barrel, round which the mainspring coils.

Beat. One vibration of the balance and spring.

Beryllium alloy. An alloy of iron, nickel, and a small percentage of beryllium, used for balance and balance spring.

Breguet spring. A balance spring in which the outer coil is raised above and carried over the body of the spring.

Bridge. Upper plates in a watch for the support of the wheels.

Butting. Two wheels touching on the points of the teeth when entering into action with each other.

Cannon pinion. The pinion with a long pipe to which the minute hand is fixed.

Center of gravity. That point in a body around which the mass is evenly balanced.

Center wheel. The wheel in a watch the axis of which usually carries the minute hand

Chronograph. A watch that has a center-seconds hand driven from the fourth wheel which can be started, stopped, and caused to fly back to zero by pressing on a knob or lever.

Chronometer. A boxed timepiece for use on ships at sea.

Chronometer escapement. A spring detent escapement used in chronometers. Invented by Pierre LeRoy about 1765

Circular escapement. An escapement so constructed that the central portion of each pallet stone's impulse face stands at an equal distance from the pallet center

Circular pitch. The pitch circle divided into as many spaces as there are teeth on the wheel or pinion.

Club-tooth wheel. That type of wheel which has a lifting face off the end of the teeth.

Clutch pinion. The pinion surrounding the square of the stem. Serves alternately to wind and set the watch

Collet. A small, circular piece fitting friction-tight to the balance staff and which is pierced to receive the inner coil of the balance spring.

Compensating balance. A balance the rim of which is made of brass and steel. The diameter is caused to increase or decrease in different temperatures, so as to compensate for changes in temperature on both balance and spring.

Corner safety test. A test to show the presence or absence of safety lock when the slot corner is brought in contact with the roller jewel.

Crescent. A circular notch in the edge of the roller table for the reception of the guard pin or finger.

Crown. A grooved circular piece fastened to the stem for winding the watch.

Crown wheel. A wheel that drives the ratchet wheel.

Curb pins. Regulator pins.

Curve test. A test used to discover if the curves of the lever horns are correctly related to the roller jewel.

Cylinder escapement. A frictional escapement patented by Thomas Tompion 1695.

Dedendum. The portion of the tooth of either wheel or pinion inside of the pitch circle.

Dial train. A train of two wheels and two pinions that control the progress of the minute hand and the hour hand.

Diametrical pitch. The diameter of the pitch circle divided into as many spaces as there are teeth on a wheel or pinion.

Discharging pallet. The pallet stone which an escape-wheel tooth slides over in order to emerge from between the pallet stones.

Distance of centers. The distance on a straight line from center to center, as between balance center and pallet center.

Double-roller escapement. A form of lever escapement in which a separate roller is used for the safety action.

Draw. A force that keeps the lever against the banking pins, created by the slant of the pallet stones.

Driven. The mobile that is being forced along by the driver.

Driver. The mobile that forces the other along.

Drop. The free motion of the escape wheel after impulse to the pallets has been given.

Drop lock. The extent of the lock on the pallets after an escapement has been banked to the drop.

Duplex escapement. A watch escapement in which the escape wheel has two sets of teeth. One set locks the wheel by pressing on the balance staff The other set gives impulse to the balance The balance receives impulse at every other vibration Accredited to Pierre LeRoy about 1750

Epicycloid. A curve generated by a point in the circumference of a circle as it rolls upon another circle. It forms the kind of tooth used in watch wheels.

Equidistant escapement. An escapement so constructed that the locking faces of the pallet stones stand at an equal distance from the pallet center

Elinvar. A nonrusting, nonmagnetizing alloy containing iron, nickel, chromium, tungsten, silicon and carbon. Used for balance and balance spring.

Fork. The horns and slot of the lever.

Fourth wheel. The wheel of a watch that drives the escape pinion.

Guard pin or finger. A pin or finger working in and out of the crescent to preserve the safety action.

Guard safety test. A test to show the presence or absence of safety lock when the guard pin or finger is brought in contact with the edge of roller.

Heel of tooth. Letting-off corner of a tooth of the escape wheel.

Horns. The circular sides of the fork leading into the slot.

Hour wheel. The wheel that carries the hour hand.

Hypocycloid. A curve generated by a point in the circumference of a circle when it is rolled within another circle.

Impulse pin. Roller jewel.

Invar. A steel alloy containing about 36 per cent nickel Used in the making of balance wheels

Isochronism. The property of a balance spring that allows it to perform the long and short arcs in equal time.

Letting-off corner. Corner of a pallet stone from which a tooth lets off.

Lever. A metal piece attached to the pallets that carries impulse to the balance.

Lever escapement. A watch escapement that delivers impulse to the balance by means of two pallet stones and a lever. The extremity of the lever has a forked slot that acts directly on a roller jewel which is attached to the balance. Invented about 1750 by Thomas Mudge.

Lift. The pitch or slant of a tooth or pallet stone.

Line of centers. A line drawn from center to center, as of any wheel or pinion.

Locking. The overlapping of a tooth on a pallet stone.

Lossier curves. The theoretical outer and inner terminals as designed by L. Lossier.

Main train. The toothed wheels in a watch that connect the barrel with the escapement.

Middle-temperature error. The temperature error between the extremes of heat and cold characteristic of a compensating balance and steel balance spring

Minute wheel. The wheel driven by the cannon pinion.

Out of angle. Unequal angular motion of the lever from the line of centers when an escapement is banked to the drop

Overbanked. A term used to indicate that the lever escapement is out of action.

Overcoil. The last coil of the Breguet spring that is bent up and over the body of the spring.

Pallet arms. The metal body which contains the pallet stones.

Pallets. The metal body attached to or a part of the lever The term includes the pallet arms and pallet stones.

Pallet staff. The axis of the pallets.

Pallet stones. Jewels or stones inserted in the pallet arms.

Phillips' spring. A balance spring with terminal curves formed on lines laid down by M. Phillips The term "Phillips' curve" is rarely used.

Pinion. The smaller wheel with teeth called leaves, working in connection with a larger wheel.

Pitch circle. A circle concentric with the circumference of a toothed wheel and cutting its teeth at such a distance from their points as to touch the corresponding circle of a pinion working with it and having with that circle a common velocity, as in a rolling contact.

Pitch diameter. The diameter of the pitch circle.

Pivot. The end of a rotating arbor.

Plate. Discs of brass or nickel which form the foundation of a movement. The lower plate lies next to the dial. The upper pieces supporting one, two, or three wheels are generally referred to as bridges. In the full-plate watch the upper piece is called the top plate.

Potence. A hang-down bracket used for supporting the lower pivot of the balance staff in full-plate watches.

Quarter screws. Four screws used in timing

Ratchet wheel. A wheel that is fastened to the barrel arbor.

Ratchet tooth wheel. The name given to the English type escape wheel which has pointed teeth.

Receiving pallet. The pallet stone over which a tooth of the escape wheel slides in order to enter between the pallet stones.

Remaining lock. The lock remaining when the guard and corner tests are tried. More often called "safety lock."

Repeater. A watch that strikes, having two hammers and two gongs A lever is provided to set the striking mechanism into action. A quarter repeater strikes the hour and the last quarter hour. A minute repeater, in addition, strikes the number of minutes since the last quarter.

Right-angled escapement. An escapement in which the line of centers of the escape wheel and pallets are at right angles to pallets and balance.

Roller jewel. A long, thin jewel inserted in the roller table; sometimes called impulse pin.

Roller table. A circular disc attached to the balance staff in which is fitted the roller jewel.

Run of lever. The motion of the lever toward the banking pins when slide is present. Run always equals slide.

Safety lock. The lock remaining when the guard and corner tests are tried.

Semitangental escapement. An escapement where the locking face of the receiving pallet is planted 31 degrees from the line of centers and the discharging pallet 29 degrees from the line of centers. The receiving pallet locks only on the tangent.

Shake. The space separating the letting-off corner of the pallet from the heel of a tooth when the opposite pallet is locked at the lowest locking corner. Shake is always less than drop.

Single roller escapement. A form of lever escapement in which one roller performs the functions of both impulse and safety actions.

Slide. The opening of the banking pins beyond that of drop lock.

Steady pins. Pins used to secure the perfect alignment of two pieces of metal.

Stem. The winding arbor of a watch.

Stop work. A mechanical device for preventing the over-winding of a mainspring.

Straight line escapement. An escapement in which the centers of the escape wheel, pallets, and balance are planted in a straight line

Stud. A small piece of metal pierced to receive the outer coil of the balance spring.

Third wheel. The wheel of a watch that drives the fourth pinion.

Timing screws. Screws used to bring a watch to time, sometimes called the mean-time screws.

Toe of tooth. Locking corner of a tooth of the escape wheel.

Total lock. Drop lock with slide added.

Train. A combination of two or more wheels and pinions, geared together and transmitting power from one part of a mechanism to another.

Tripping. A tooth of the escape wheel running past the locking face of a pallet stone at a time when safety lock should be present.

Wheel. Any circular piece of metal on the periphery of which teeth may be cut of various forms and numbers.

Winding pinions. A pinion surrounding the stem that drives the crown wheel.

BIBLIOGRAPHY

WATCHES

Borer and Bowman,
   Modern Watch Repairing and Adjusting

DeCarle, Donald,
   With the Watchmaker at the Bench

Garrard, F. J.,
   Watch Repairing, Cleaning and Adjusting

Gribi, Theo.,
   Practical Course in Adjusting

Grossman, Jules and Herman,
   Lessons in Horology

Hood, Grant,
   Modern Methods in Horology

Kleinlein, Walter J.,
   Rules and Practice in Adjusting Watches
   Practical Balance and Hairspring Work

Thisell, A. G.,
   Watch Repairing Simplified

Wilkinson, T. J.,
   The Escapement and Train of American Watches

WATCHES AND CLOCKS

Britten, F. J.,
Watch and Clock Makers' Handbook

Haswell, Eric,
Horology

Saunier, Claudius,
Treatise on Modern Horology

CLOCKS

Garrard, F. J.,
Clock Making and Repairing

Gordon, G. F. C.,
Clock Making, Past and Present

Langman and Ball,
Electrical Horology

Philpott, Stuart F.,
Modern Electric Clocks

Robinson, T. R.,
Modern Clocks, Their Repair and Adjustment

HISTORY

Britten, F. J.,
Old Watches and Clocks and Their Makers

Chamberlin, Paul M.,
It's About Time

Gould, Rupert T.,
The Marine Chronometer, Its History and Development

Hering, D. W.,
  The Lure of the Clock

Nutting, Wallace,
  The Clock Book

ALLIED SUBJECTS

Bennett, Charles A ,
  Beginning Problems in Mechanical Drawing

Eaton and Free,
  Machine Shop Science and Mathematics

Feirer and Williams,
  Basic Electricity

McMackin and Shaver,
  Mathematics of the Shop

Roberts, William E.,
  Beginning Mechanical Drawing

INDEX

A

B

185

CPSIA information can be obtained
at www.ICGtesting.com
Printed in the USA
LVOW13s0538251017
553666LV00011BA/258/P